Power and Movement

Power and Movement

Portraits of Britain's Paralympic Athletes

Photography by Richard Booth

Text by Debbie Beckerman

WILEY

FSC
www.fsc.org
MIX
Paper from
responsible sources
FSC® C015829

CONTENTS

To all the Paralympic athletes I have worked with in preparing this book, with best wishes for their future success.

p.2 Liz Johnson, who won gold at Beijing 2008 in the 100m Breaststroke, was only 14 when she became part of the British Paralympic Swimming team. In 2011 she was invited to place the last of 180,000 tiles in the Aquatics Centre for the London 2012 Olympic and Paralympic Games, where she hopes to repeat her success. 'I've got the taste for gold, and I won't be short of motivation to land another one in 2012.'

p.5 At 19, Kyron Duke's international career has already spanned two sports. He represented Wales in powerlifting at the Commonwealth Games in 2010, and the following year turned to track and field for the World Championships in New Zealand, where he won a bronze medal in the javelin competition. He now has the London 2012 Paralympic Games firmly in his sights. 'Being able to compete on home turf and in front of a home crowd would be brilliant and it would really spur me on.'

p.7 Sarah Storey has won Paralympic gold medals in both Swimming and Cycling events, most recently at Beijing 2008. She relishes the opportunities that her success has brought and is a committed patron of two charities.

p.14 Tom Hall-Butcher, who also enjoys playing wheelchair basketball, has developed the mental and physical strength to take on the best wheelchair fencers in the world. 'I like being part of a squad and of the fencing family.'

INTRODUCTION BY RICHARD BOOTH

In May 2011 I was working in Weymouth, on Britain's south coast. It was blowing a gale out on the boat, with winds up to 30 knots, and I was struggling to shoot some of Great Britain's finest Paralympic sailors. This was one of the trickiest shoots of the entire project and the weather was not exactly helping. However, as I reflected back on what had brought me to this point, I was determined to get it right, however long it took to get the images I was looking for.

I have always had a passion for sport and for creative photography. In addition, through one of my commercial clients, I had helped to raise money for the British Olympic Association (BOA) and the British Paralympic Association (BPA). Soon after that I met, and began to photograph, some exceptional Paralympic athletes, including swimmer Kate Grey, fencer Tom Hall-Butcher and athlete Libby Clegg. I was inspired by the sheer drive and energy they showed. It dovetailed perfectly with the style and dynamism of the images that I was developing for this sporting portfolio.

By this time, the London Organising Committee of the Olympic and Paralympic Games (LOCOG) had become involved and I had also met the Vice-Chair of the BPA, Ann Cutcliffe. She shared with me a determination to redefine traditional perceptions of disability, fitness and power. We had the same vision: to celebrate the skill, expertise and beauty of Paralympic athletes. The final stage was to secure a partnership with John Wiley, one of the official publishers for London 2012, who commissioned me to produce all the photographs for this book. The brief was to capture the extraordinary journeys of these individuals, including their aspirations and motivation as they moved towards their goal of taking part in the London 2012 Paralympic Games.

I began work on the project in December 2010. This first involved a lot of research on the sports themselves. Some, such as Boccia, Goalball and Football 5-a-side for visually-impaired athletes,

Left: Boccia champion David Smith enjoys the opportunity to demonstrate his skill.

British sailors John Robertson, Stephen Thomas and Hannah Stodel sailing in the mixed Sonar class in Weymouth in May 2011.

are unique to the Paralympic Games and I admit I knew little about them. Gaining an understanding of each of the 20 sports to be covered was essential, so the photographs could show these very varied disciplines to best advantage. There was also much to organise in advance of the shoots. I had to plan (and on occasion re-plan) a shooting schedule, involving constant contact with PRs, coaches and sometimes the athletes themselves. At times there were logistical challenges, as these are all, understandably, very busy people. Athletes are frequently away competing and are based in a huge variety of locations around Britain. In total I travelled over 40,000 kilometres. From Glasgow and Sheffield, via Nottingham, Loughborough, Staffordshire, Cardiff, and through to London, the South East of England and Weymouth, there is almost no part of the country that I did not travel through during the six months that it took to complete this project.

Sometimes, I was given a choice of dates for a shoot, or advance warning of where and when I could photograph the athletes in question. On other occasions, because of their training and competition schedules, I would be told, as I was with wheelchair tennis, 'Our top guys are playing week in week out, and are available for one day at the end of February – is that OK?' Wheelchair tennis is a global sport and Peter Norfolk, one of its stars, is understandably not often in town. When it came to the shoot, Peter, being a very driven character, said we had five minutes. I decided to shoot to a laptop so that he could immediately see the images of him we were capturing. This seemed to do the trick because 30 minutes later we were only just packing up. However, just before we did, I thought I'd ask him to play a final shot close to my camera. His aim was perfect: he got so close that he hit my tripod, just an inch below my £25,000 camera. A heart-stopping moment – although some might say it served me right for pushing my luck!

The shoots began in earnest in January, during heavy snowfalls and downpours of rain. First off was table tennis in Sheffield, followed by a total contrast, equestrian, with nine-time Paralympic gold medallist Lee Pearson in Staffordshire. Soon after, it was up to Glasgow for my introduction to boccia via the brothers Stephen and Peter McGuire, two of the funniest and most brilliant

Wheelchair tennis ace Peter Norfolk powers a ball straight towards the camera.

characters in the game. Nothing was too much trouble, and they generously gave me three precious hours of their time. I didn't know much about the technicalities of boccia beforehand, but it was inspiring to meet them both, and to witness their competitiveness even if it was during a set-up photo shoot. And luckily, being half Scottish, I immediately got their sense of humour.

Every athlete is, by definition, unique, and it was important for me to try to convey their personalities through the images. It sometimes took a little time for them to understand what I was aiming for. Some of them imagined that I would just be turning up, clicking away for 10 minutes, then going away. It was only when they saw me setting up double sets of lights that they realised these were not going to be ordinary photo shoots.

I have always said it doesn't matter what you shoot on, be it digital, film or throw-away, as long as you see it and shoot it. But for this project I needed the very best of what camera and lighting manufacturers could give me. When it came to lighting, about which I am passionate, I used a mix of very fast flash, to capture the frozen motion, and continuous Tungsten lights, to capture the flow and energy; these gave me everything I wanted in the images, and I then used either long or very fast shutter speeds. For the camera, I had decided that I wanted to show every nuance of the athlete in motion. This led me to use the same equipment that I use

Nine-times Paralympic Games gold medallist Lee Pearson, saying hello to his horse, Gentleman.

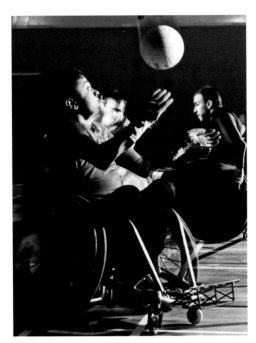

Wheelchair rugby player Bulbul Hussain, training hard in the run-up to London 2012.

for my advertising imagery, as it gave me the control I needed as well as the knowledge that I could throw everything at the athletes and get what I wanted. You wouldn't normally see big medium-format digital cameras in the sports arena as you only get one image every few seconds – a mile away from the press cameras of today that can shoot 40 frames per second and simply capture what is in front of them.

By using the former type of camera, I had to anticipate when it was going to react and what the athlete was going to do – not always the easiest thing to time and get right. This was especially true when I was having to set up the shot

and ask the athletes to do and re-do the movement several times to get it just right; their helpful co-operation was hugely appreciated. However, I really did not want to retouch the images, so the ones in the book are all 'straight out of the camera', except for a bit of dust clean-up and colour conversion.

There were weather and location considerations to take into account every time. There were also the physical difficulties in getting into the right position to capture the essence of the sport and the athlete. When we shot the riders, for example, we had to do so in such a way that we would not frighten the horses. When we photographed the rifle and pistol shooters, we had to capture the focus and precision of a static sport whilst at the same time showing its power and energy. And when we shot the sailors, we had to go out on a boat alongside them in what were appalling conditions. In the end some of the images had to be taken during an international regatta (the only ones in the book taken during a competition), because we had already waited two days to get even remotely clement weather.

Time was often tight for each shoot, so I had to have an image already in mind of what I was aiming for before I arrived and without fully knowing the location or the weather – or even which athlete would be there on the day. Once I started, though, they all behaved like true professionals and took direction extremely well, often involving themselves enthusiastically in

the whole process, making sure the action and positions were right and that I was capturing their sport correctly. All along, I have aimed to include as wide a variety of athletes as possible in this project, from elite Paralympians such as Lee Pearson (Equestrian, nine golds), David Roberts (Swimming, 11 golds), Jody Cundy (Cycling and Swimming, five golds), Sarah Storey (Cycling and Swimming, seven golds) and David Weir (Athletics, two golds) to exciting new talented sportsmen and women who are doing everything in their power to compete at London 2012. Inevitably, reasons of space mean that not everyone can be featured, but I will

European, World Championship and Paralympic Games gold medallist Deb Criddle on her horse, LTK Akilles.

John Stubbs, who won a gold medal in the Paralympic Archery competition at Beijing 2008, takes aim, his focus firmly on the London 2012 Paralympic Games.

never forget any of the shoots and the remarkable athletes that I met at them. Thank you to you all.

I must pay tribute to people whose help, input and support have been invaluable in making this book possible. Due to time constraints I worked with three different assistants on this project, and must thank each of them for bringing their own muscle and humour to the shoots. I have worked with both James and Brendan for so many years that it becomes easy; and Shaun, you slotted in well! It was an extremely physical job. We sometimes worked in excess of 20 hours a day, carrying lots of lights and camera equipment – we tended to have about 150–200 kilograms of equipment on any

one shoot – so there were a few amusing reactions when we turned up and it just kept coming out of the vehicles.

I also never realised how exhausting it would be to try to organise over 100 very diverse athletes from 20 different sports to be photographed, so I must thank Sarah who, alongside me, helped to arrange and diarise the shoots. I must also thank Siona, Kessia and Alana for their support, and for being so understanding when I hardly saw them for the first three months of the year.

Through the pages of this book, I have tried to offer a perspective on the athletes' personalities and their sport, and how these combine to form a whole image. The power and athleticism that

can be seen when photographed in this way is immense. Equally, the beauty and calmness of mind prior to the competition itself is wonderful to witness. I have managed to open the eyes of my family and children to Paralympic sport, and I sincerely hope that this book will now show to others how many amazingly talented athletes we have within ParalympicsGB and how much they have achieved so far. I wish all of them every success, both at the London 2012 Paralympic Games and beyond.

Gallery

ATHLETICS

Queen of Speed

Nikki Emerson took up athletics in 2009, shortly after becoming a wheelchair user. A year later she came fourth in the London Marathon.
She relishes being fit, strong and fast, and sees herself not as a disabled person but as an athlete. She has always been highly competitive and driven, and loves nothing better than pitching herself down the steepest hill she can find: 'I'm a massive adrenaline junkie.' Nikki graduated from Oxford University in 2009 with a degree in Neuroscience and Psychology and, after initially working for London 2012 as a Licensing Executive, she decided to train full time to give herself the best chance of doing well at the London 2012 Paralympic Games. For Nikki, the travelling is the best bit about being an athlete, as she gets to meet so many interesting people and to train and compete in amazing places.

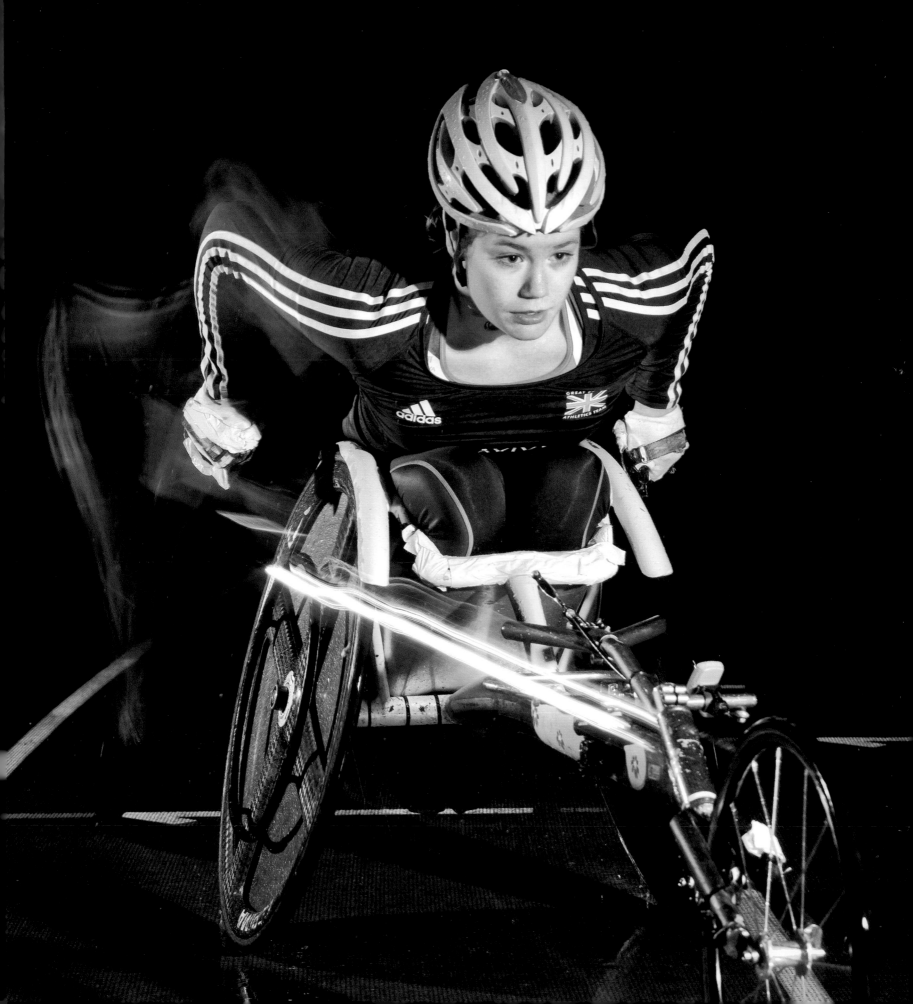

'It's an incredible feeling to be going at over 40mph with your face just a foot above the ground.'

Nikki Emerson

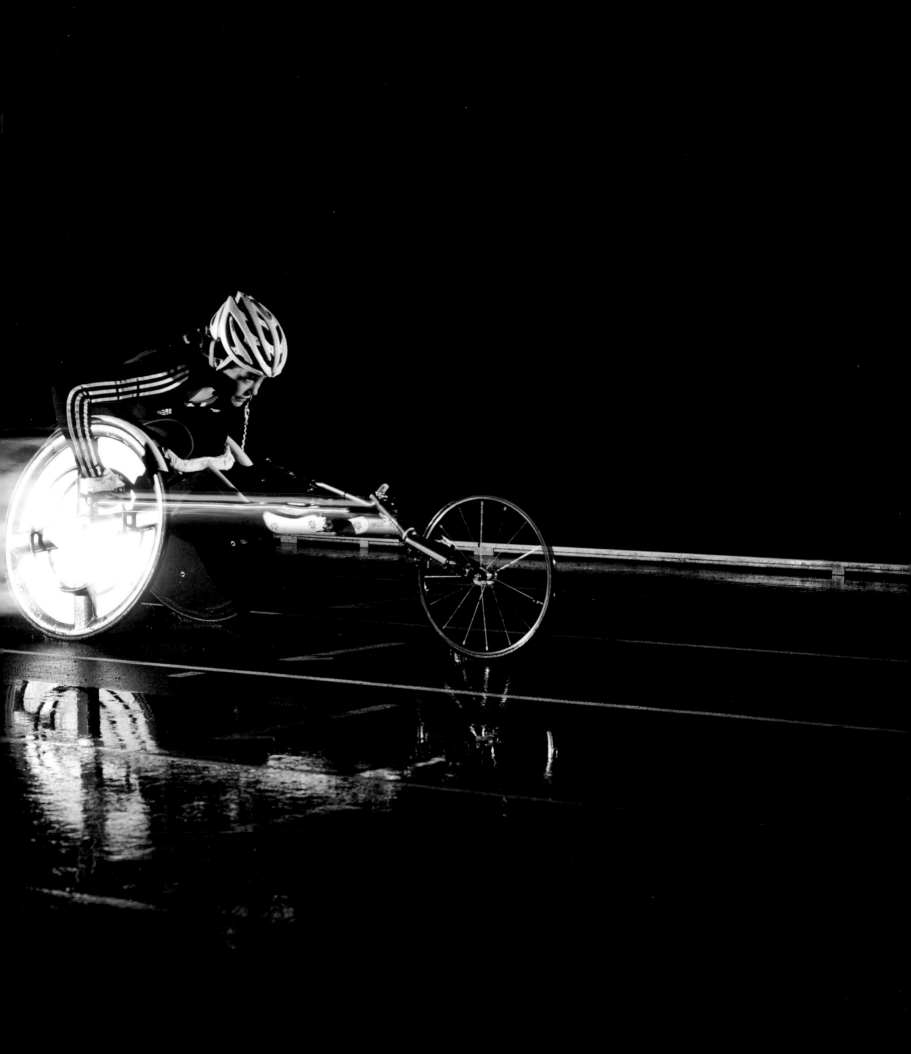

Winning Wheels

Born in 1979, David Weir MBE is one of the
most successful Paralympic athletes in history.
He currently holds the British record at all track
distances up to 5000m, as well as on the road
at 10km, half marathon and marathon. He is
also a double-gold medallist from the Beijing
2008 Paralympic Games. David always means
business – a ruthless 'local hero', he is determined
to triumph in his own back yard as he has across
the world. Given his total dedication to his sport,
it is not surprising that his sporting idol is David
Beckham – a family man like himself, who is still
committed to football despite his huge success. Away
from the track, David relaxes by DJing, listening to
house music and watching Arsenal play.

From School to Stadium

Jenny McLoughlin competes in the 100m and 200m sprint events. At just 16 years old, and having just finished her GCSEs, she was one of the youngest members of the ParalympicsGB team at Beijing 2008. Competing in those Paralympic Games remains for Jenny her greatest achievement to date. Recent successes have included a silver medal at the 2010 Commonwealth Games and double gold at the IWAS World Junior Championships 2011. In her spare time, Jenny, who follows many sports, enjoys horse riding and supports Manchester United FC. She is currently studying Philosophy at Cardiff University and is also an ambassador for the Sparkle Appeal, a charity that raises funds for a specialist centre in South Gwent for children with complex disabilities.

New Horizons

James Ledger, seen here closest to the camera, knows how important athletics has been in his life so far: 'It has given me a lot of confidence and independence.' He also acknowledges that sport has enhanced his social skills and enabled him to mix with a wide range of people whom he would not normally have got to meet. James is one of Britain's rising stars and he pays tribute to his school, which has been very supportive of him, allowing him time off whenever necessary in order to train and compete at events such as the UK School Games and the World Junior Championships in Colorado. Encouraged all the way by his friends and family, James has combined sport with studying for A levels and travelling the world for his athletics – something that has not always been easy.

'I don't think I face a lot of challenges.' Although her condition is such that she is now only able to train and compete in the visually-impaired category, when she was younger, she also ran without a guide in non-disabled races. Libby, who has three younger siblings to whom she is very close, is very sporty. She loves swimming and rugby, but is now training full time and concentrating on going one better at London 2012 than she did in Beijing 2008, when she came away with a silver medal in the 100m - T12. Libby also works unpaid for the Royal Blind Charity and for Champions in Schools, which sends top athletes to visit schools in Scotland in a bid to inspire children to take up sport.

True Grit on the Track

If she was a character in a film, Bethany Woodward would choose Lara Croft, because she's similarly strong-willed, she knows what she wants and won't stop until she gets it. Bethany likes athletics – she runs the 200m and 400m – because she can push herself to the maximum, something she says that, as a disabled person, can sometimes be difficult to do as much as she might like. Her ability to keep going, as well as her endurance levels and technique, make her a tough competitor. Bethany, who was born in 1992, left home aged 17 so that she could live near her training base at Lee Valley Athletics Centre. She is now training full time to maximise her chances of competing at London 2012.

Media Strongman

Welshman Owain Taylor competes in the javelin throw, discus throw and shot put. In 2010 he won double gold at the International Wheelchair and Amputees Sport Federation (IWASF) Junior Athletics World Championships, and is now competing at senior international level and aiming for the London 2012 Paralympic Games. Owain, who suffered a stroke when he was two, says that 'The disability has made me who I am. I wouldn't want to be able-bodied.'

He is training as a technical assistant at Able Radio, which he loves, but is devoting himself as much as possible to his athletics career.

Going the Distance

Ashleigh Hellyer used to be a sprinter but the sports-mad Swansea athlete tried out a number of other sports at the Disability Sport Wales Academy and impressed at throwing events. He was asked if he would have a go at shot put, and he immediately threw a qualifying distance. After five months of hard training and support from coaches at the Academy, Ashleigh took part in his first British and international competitions and, in the Commonwealth Games in Delhi in October 2010, he reached the final and achieved a fifth place in the shot put competition. Talking about his motivation, he says 'I just go out and throw as far as I can, I don't worry about anyone else'. His big ambition is to compete at London 2012 and to keep on improving his personal bests. 'One day, I'd love to reach over 10m and be the best in the world.'

Onward and Upward

Hollie Arnold was just 14 years old when she competed in the Javelin Throw at the Beijing 2008 Paralympic Games. The experience in China was unforgettable for her, she says, both inside and away from the Bird's Nest Stadium. Despite a stress fracture in her back the following year, Hollie has progressed in leaps and bounds since then and caught up fast with the top senior javelin throwers in the world. She moved from her home near Grimsby in 2010 in order to train with her new coach in Cardiff so that she can be as prepared as possible for London 2012.

Hunting Success

When he is not training, Nathan Stephens loves
nothing more than going away with his friends
for a weekend of surfing along the Pembrokeshire
coast. At home on the beach, he says 'I should
have been a marine biologist – I love the sea'.
Nathan, who throws both the discus and the
javelin, is now specialising in the latter and
enjoying growing success in the event. Having
come fourth at the Beijing 2008 Paralympic
Games, even though he wasn't expected to get
close to a medal position, he now cannot wait for
London 2012. A cinema fan, Nathan's favourite
throwing scene in a film is in *Troy*, when Brad
Pitt launches a spear straight over a character's
shoulder, it flies through the air for ages, then
finally knocks another soldier off his horse.
'It's ridiculous,' laughs Nathan, 'no one can
throw a javelin like that. Or that far.'

'This year was the best season I have had yet ... I am hoping to have a really good winter now and get as close as I can to my two goals for next season.'

Josh Clark

A Powerful Focus

Shot putter Josh Clark is driven by his dream of competing for Great Britain at London 2012. For Josh, who recently won a bronze medal at the IWAS World Junior Championships in Dubai, his biggest achievement so far is representing his country in sport: 'Nothing tops that'. He takes every competition as it comes, likes to keep himself to himself, and simply gets on with the business of doing as well as he possibly can. He first got involved in sport when his school had a sports day at the same stadium in Wales where the Welsh Paralympic team were training. Selected for the shot put that day, he was spotted by a coach and asked if he wanted to get involved in disability sport. Since that day, Josh hasn't looked back.

Poetry in Motion

Dan Greaves believes that throwing the discus
is like an art form. He explains that, as well as
having agility and good orientation, a good
discus thrower needs to take into account other
elements, such as the wind, the weather and the
aerodynamics of the throw. It's so hard to get right
that when he does, he finds it immensely satisfying.
Dan is a Paralympic gold medallist in Discus
Throw (at Athens 2004) and has also competed
internationally as a non-disabled athlete. He is
competitive and highly motivated in life and in
his sport, and remembers the thrill of beating his
classmates at school when he first took up the
discus in his mid-teens. Dan's other passion is
Aston Villa, to which he has a season ticket, and
although he trains full time, he also enjoys going
to the cinema with his girlfriend, and meeting up
with friends whenever he can.

Throwing for Gold

Vicky Silk only started athletics seriously in 2006 at Ashford Athletics Club, but has since won numerous medals at international events, including, most notably, gold at the IWAS Junior Athletics World Championships in 2010 and 2011. She says that it takes a lot of determination and focus to set and achieve her personal goals, which, in addition to her sport, have included passing her A-levels to secure her university place. She has had to make a lot of sacrifices and give up a lot of free time to train and compete, but is reaping the rewards of all her hard work and hopes to fulfil her dream of competing at the London 2012 Paralympic Games.

Reaping Rewards

Josie Pearson created history at Beijing 2008, by becoming the first woman Wheelchair Rugby player to compete for Britain at the Paralympic Games. Since then, she has switched over to athletics and become one of Great Britain's top Paralympic athletes. She encourages anyone to have a go at sport, whatever their ability and no matter what level they want to reach, because it can bring them so much both mentally and physically, saying 'sport has improved my day-to-day life in terms of my confidence'. In her bid to inspire others, Josie helped to launch Talent 2012: Paralympic Potential, a nationwide talent search for athletes of all disciplines. Josie, who had begun a degree in Neuroscience at Cardiff University but decided after the first year to concentrate full time on her sporting career, says that thanks to sport, she has had the best experiences of her life.

Keeping a Balance

Dan West's parents encouraged him into athletics and, although he tried team sports such as football, which he loves, he chose the shot put (he also used to compete internationally in the discus throw) because he likes the fact that it's all down to him whether he does well or not. The shot put is a powerful event, requiring excellent technique to get the shot moving from a static position. Dan is fast and strong with long arms, and this gives him an edge. He has competed in four Paralympic Games, from Atlanta 1996 to Beijing 2008, and he has won medals in three of them. When Dan gave up work to train full time a few years ago, he put himself under too much pressure. Based in Loughborough, he now chooses to work part time and he says that this, together with his wife, keeps him grounded.

SPEED SPORTS

A Natural Winner

Sarah Storey is a multiple medal-winning athlete.
As well as numerous world titles, she won five
Paralympic gold medals in Swimming before
switching to Cycling and winning two gold
medals at Beijing 2008. Not surprisingly, she was
awarded the OBE soon after. She describes herself
as naturally a very driven person, and, because
her body has been through a lot physically, she
has learnt how to get the best out of herself and
as a result to have a great capacity for training,
however gruelling. She loves it all, though.
'What's not to love, doing the job you most want
to do?' Sarah is also patron of two charities,
The Children's Adventure Farm Trust and Boot
Out Breast Cancer, and devotes as much spare
time as she can to both causes.

'Being an athlete is a real privilege and I thank my lucky stars every day.'

Sarah Storey

Driven to Win

Rachel Morris used to be a keen runner and dreamt of appearing at the Olympic Games. When a rare illness resulted in her having both legs amputated, Rachel took up handcycling as a way of controlling the pain by releasing endorphins into her bloodstream. 'Handcycling is more than a sport to me ... It is a way of managing the pain ... And it's what I do – it's what I get up to in the morning, it's what I go to bed at night thinking about – it is me.' Rachel made her competitive debut in 2006 and, as well as becoming a multiple gold-winning World Champion in the intervening years, she won Individual Time Trial gold at the Beijing 2008 Paralympic Games. Rachel trains full time, twice a day, and is out on the roads for hours, which can be highly dangerous. When she is not cycling, Rachel loves to sail: she is an accomplished sailor and competes at international level.

'I've got to think of London 2012. That is the ultimate goal for everyone and the pinnacle of my career so I do have to be careful … the Games have so much power and so much emotion that does drive me on.'

Rachel Morris

Chasing Victory

Jody Cundy MBE has won 10 World
Championship titles and five Paralympic gold
medals in two different sports. After a 10-year
career in swimming, Jody took up cycling in
2005 and achieved instant success. He is always
striving to reach the next level in his sport and to
demonstrate what is possible with an impairment.
'When I train on the track, in most sessions I'm on
with people like Chris Hoy and Victoria Pendleton
... it's hugely inspiring,' he's said. He loves the
motorbike chases he does at the velodrome as
part of his training, when he reaches speeds of
75km/h. The white-knuckle ride is exhilarating,
and the sense of speed addictive.

Heroes on Bikes

Jon-Allan Butterworth (shown here cycling nearest to the camera) lost his arm in a rocket attack in 2007 while serving with the RAF in Iraq and has a tattoo on his chest with the date and GPS coordinates of where and when he got injured, near a scar left by the bomb. He took up cycling after his injury, and quickly achieved success, including setting a world record and winning a gold medal in the 1km time trial at the 2011 World Track Championships in Italy. Pictured left, below Terry Byrne, Jon-Allan thrives on the sensation of speed and adrenaline when riding his bike.

Terry Byrne (cycling furthest from the camera), a Corporal in the 2nd Battalion Parachute Regiment, lost his leg below the knee after stepping on a landmine in Afghanistan in August 2008. It was while watching the Beijing 2008 Paralympic Games during his stay in Birmingham's Selly Oak Hospital that he decided to take up cycling, helped by the Battle Back programme that assists wounded service personnel back to an active life. His gold medal in his first World Track Championships in 2011 is a testament to his will to win and to his fitness. Having served his country once, he wants to serve his country again in London 2012 and make his family proud.

One of Cycling's Brightest Stars

Darren Kenny OBE is a six-time Paralympic
gold medallist who has also won 16 World Cup
golds. He admits that he does not like the training
at all; it mainly consists of long hours of pain
and suffering, but it serves a purpose. Highly
competitive, Darren relishes the challenge of his
accomplished Paralympic teammates (above).
He can't bear the thought of being second best
and is always aiming to do the perfect ride. He
claims that good genetics and having the best
coach have enabled him to achieve so much
in his career, and can demonstrate that being
vegetarian since childhood has clearly not
slowed him down.

Tandem Express

Aileen McGlynn OBE recalls wondering as a child what she would do when she grew up because she didn't think she could continue her passion, which was cycling. Although she has a degree in Maths, Statistics and Management Science and worked as a trainee actuary for nine years, Aileen feels very fortunate because she is able to devote herself full time to cycling. After winning a gold medal at Athens 2004, she took two further golds and set a new world record at Beijing 2008. Aileen is now looking forward to defending her titles at London 2012.

Tandems are heavier than a solo bike, so Helen Scott, who is the pilot for Aileen McGlynn, gets a buzz out of riding fast into the velodrome bankings, gaining speed, and letting the banking whip them round and out again. 'I love the feeling of the tandem when we are going fast!' Helen was a successful young sprinter but decided in 2010 to switch from being a solo rider to a tandem pilot. She is proud of how she handled the transition and is now thriving in her new discipline, winning a silver medal in her first World Championships.

EQUESTRIAN

A Powerful Partnership

'It's all about the feel,' according to nine-times Paralympic Equestrian gold medallist Lee Pearson, CBE. Lee, shown here on his horse Gentleman, has represented Great Britain at the Sydney 2000, Athens 2004 and Beijing 2008 Paralympic Games. Horses give Lee freedom, movement and energy, and whether he is training or riding them, Lee works above all with their personality, using his communication skills. He constantly adjusts to their needs, doing whatever is necessary to suit each individual horse, using feel to get the very best out of them. Lee's passion for all things equestrian means that he is constantly fine-tuning technical aspects in his quest for perfection. One of Great Britain's most successful and biggest sporting personalities, Lee also thrives on adrenaline, both from riding and pursuing his other obsession – driving fast cars and quad bikes to the edge of their capacity.

Saddling up for Success

Jo Pitt cannot imagine life without horses. She comes from a riding background and was taught as a non-disabled rider from a young age. As well as dressage, she also did jumping and cross-country and was always determined to keep up with non-disabled riders. If she fell off, which she frequently did, she simply got straight back on again. All this early experience paid off because it improved her balance and coordination, kept her calm when things didn't go her way and strengthened her determination to keep improving. Her motivation comes from the satisfaction of competing for her country in Paralympic Equestrian events combined with her love of riding and training great horses such as Estralita, pictured here.

A Tower of Strength

Born in 1948, Anne Dunham MBE is hoping London 2012 will mark her fifth consecutive appearance in the Equestrian events at a Paralympic Games. She first competed at the Atlanta 1996 Paralympic Games, and has won a total of seven medals, including five golds. Her motivation comes not so much from competing against others but from competing against herself, improving on what she's already achieved, and never taking anything for granted. Stubbornness and strength of mind are two of her defining characteristics, so she's always pushing herself physically and mentally. This keeps her fitter as well as mentally more agile. Anne did not own her own horse until she was in her mid-40s, and before then rode any horse she was able to. This has made her very adaptable and able to read a horse quickly, and is part of the secret of her success. She is shown here on her horse Teddy Edwards, with whom she won gold in Beijing 2008.

The Stuff of Dreams

Born in 1990, Sophie Wells grew up on a farm and started riding Shetland ponies at the age of two. She is the youngest member of the GB Paralympic Equestrian squad, and is the first-ever para-equestrian rider to have competed internationally on both the non-disabled Great Britain junior team and the para-equestrian senior team. In 2010, she took part in several junior international competitions, while also winning a para-equestrian gold medal at the World Equestrian Games. Shown here with Reece, Sophie loves the connection she has with her horses and believes that it is the unique partnership she creates with them that brings about results in competitions. That and her dreams: 'You have to have dreams to achieve anything, otherwise there's no ambition.'

A World Class Winner

Emma Sheardown, who was born with cerebral palsy, has been riding since she was two years old, when her physiotherapist suggested to her parents that it would help her physical development. By the age of 10, wanting to progress with her riding, she started para-equestrian dressage to compete. She moved on to dressage competitions by the age of 16, before becoming part of the World Class Para-Equestrian Dressage Development Squad in 2004. In October 2010, she won gold in the Freestyle 1a event at the World Equestrian Games in the USA, saying with disbelief, 'somehow I'm a World Equestrian Games gold medallist!' Riding is her life, and she loves all the hours of training (seen here seated with her horse, Eddie, and Karen Thompson, standing) which involve mainly riding but also some gym work. She hopes to fulfil her dream of winning a gold medal at the London 2012 Paralympic Games.

Freedom and Fellowship

Felicity Coulthard, seen here with Roffelaar, has been riding since she was a young girl. She enjoys the unique feeling of mental freedom that riding gives her, allowing her to get away from everything. She has been on the World Class Development Programme since 2005 and, after winning a silver medal at the Beijing 2008 Paralympic Games, is aiming to compete at London 2012. She spends two days a week in competition training, but also enjoys simply hacking because it's a good break from competing. She loves getting together with the rest of the Paralympic Equestrian squad, thanks to the great team spirit that exists amongst her fellow riders. But above all, she loves being a mum to her son Ethan, born in 2010.

Trust and Teamwork

Sophie Christiansen MBE has always loved sport and is highly competitive. However, her ambition is balanced by enormous empathy for her horse, Robin, and a complete understanding of him. She feels this comes from knowing her own limitations, giving her an instinctive awareness of how much she can ask of him. She will not push him to do what he's uncomfortable with or unable to do. In return, she knows her horse gives everything he has for her. This sense of partnership was instilled in her by her trainer for the last 10 years, Clive Milkins, who says, 'It takes team work to make a dream work.' Sophie won three medals at the Beijing 2008 Paralympic Games, two gold and one silver, and was awarded an MBE in the 2009 New Year's Honours List for services to disabled sport. She has recently graduated with a first-class Masters in Maths from the University of London, and is hoping to build on her Paralympic Games success at London 2012.

POWER SPORTS

Pumping Iron in the Powerlift

Aged only six, Ali Jawad decided he wanted to win a gold medal at the Paralympic Games. It took him a while to find the right sport. Initially, he competed at an international level in judo, but in the last few years he has dedicated himself to powerlifting and took part in the Beijing 2008 Paralympic Games aged just 18. He enjoys lifting the massive weights and the sense of pride he gets when he achieves his own targets. So far, he has won World and European junior titles and set several European junior records. Ali is a student in London but is training full time for London 2012, which he hopes very much to take part in. When training goes well, he is the happiest person alive, according to him; when it goes badly, he is very miserable and shouldn't be approached.

'My ambition is to be the greatest. I have a long way to go but I think I'm capable of it.'

Ali Jawad

A Golden Goal

Natalie Blake describes herself as 'friendly, outgoing, helpful', but in 2011 she was also ranked in the top six powerlifters in the world for her category. She is a three-time Paralympian, narrowly missing out on medals at Sydney 2000, Athens 2004 and Beijing 2008. Having taken up powerlifting in 1999 after switching from athletics, at 18 she was the youngest member of the ParalympicsGB Powerlifting squad at the Sydney 2000 Paralympic Games. Indeed, entering the Olympic Stadium for the Opening Ceremony of the Paralympic Games remains her most memorable sporting moment. Her ambition is to win a gold medal at London 2012, and although she likes to socialise with friends when she is not training or competing, the demands of her sport are such that she would advise anyone thinking of taking up powerlifting to a high level to think carefully because, as she says, 'it's a lot of hard work!'

A Force for the Future

Roxan Luckock, who was born in 1992, took up powerlifting in 2007, but didn't get the buzz of competition straight away. However, her mother's death 18 months later, when Roxan was just 16, was a turning point for her, and she decided to make something positive out of such a traumatic event. Her hard work paid off and, thanks in part to her enormous willpower and determination, she became Under-18 World Powerlifting Champion in the 48kg category in 2010. Roxan says that when she wins, her mum is constantly with her. She also appreciates her family and friends more, and although they have had to accept that her sport is the priority in her life, she likes to spend quality time with them whenever she can.

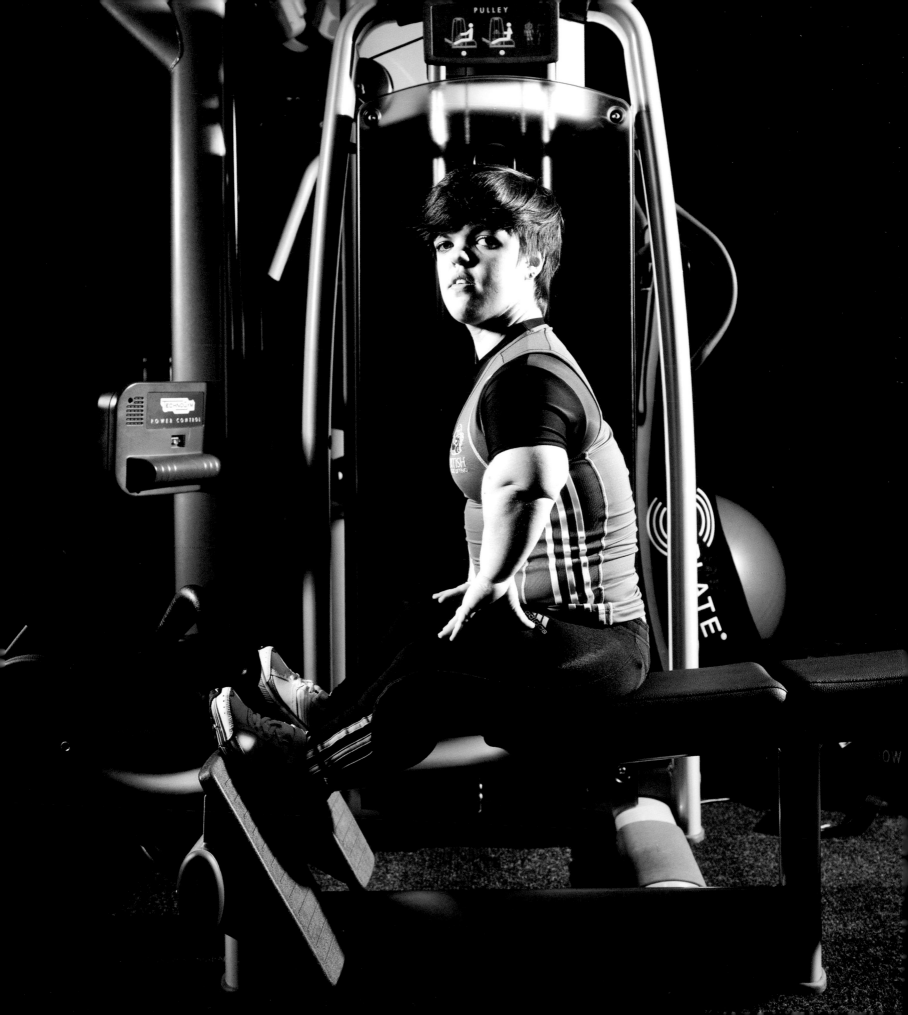

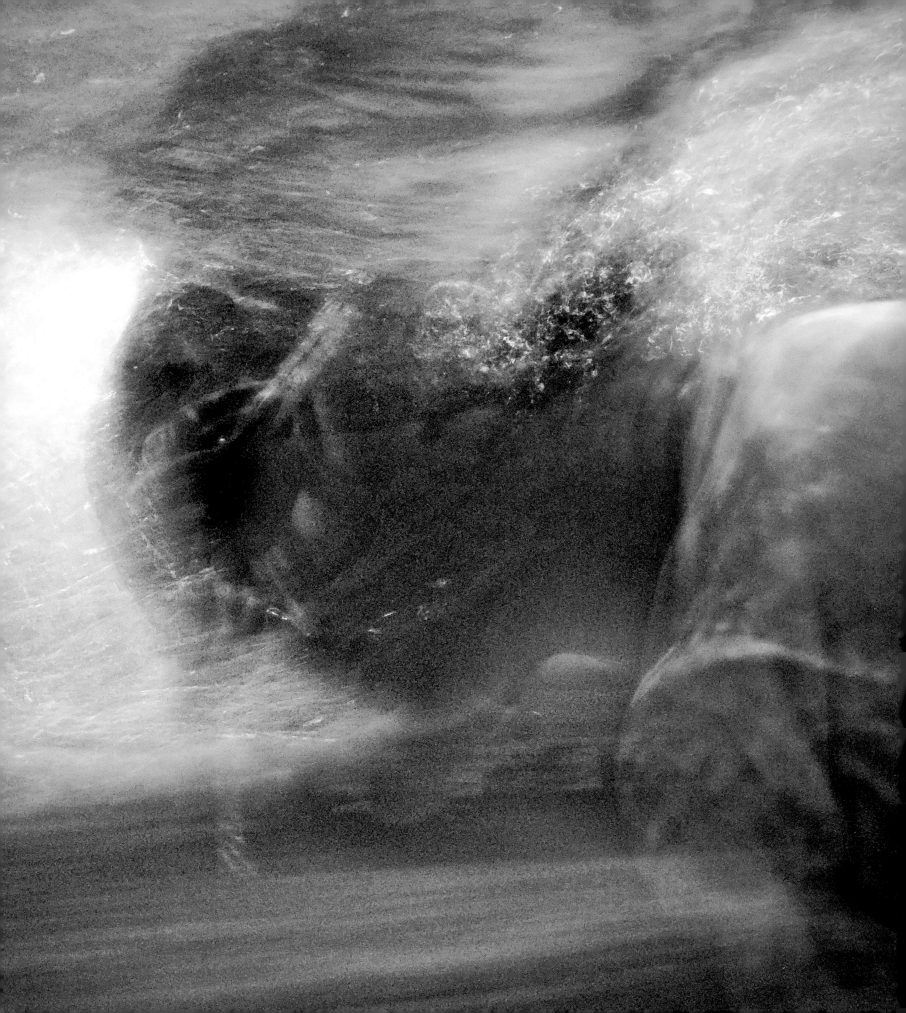

WATER SPORTS

Life in the Fast Lane

Kate Grey just missed out on a medal at the Beijing 2008 Games, and her desire to get on the podium at London 2012 drives her to train for five hours a day, mostly in the pool. She obviously loves the work, saying 'If I have a couple of days off from training, I get bored.' As a youngster, she competed in non-disabled netball, riding and athletics, and only concentrated on swimming aged 17. She has really good starts, which is vital for her sprint event, the 100m Breaststroke, and thinks that competing in other sports contributed to her having strong legs. When she was a student at Bath University she used her time in the pool to think about her next essay. Nowadays she puts on a song before she starts her training; it swirls around in her head as she does her laps, and this stops her from overthinking her stroke.

‘The most incredible experience …
I believe I can do anything now.’

Kate Grey

Mind Over Matter

Psychology and Sports Studies graduate Charlotte Henshaw is a huge musical theatre fan, whose favourite productions are *Les Miserables* and *Wicked*. She currently does not have much opportunity to indulge her passion, however, as she is devoting all her time to intense training. There are no easy roads to swimming success, according to Charlotte. You can't get lucky, you simply have to put in the hours. She has always swum competitively, so she is used to the hours of swimming required, and she likes the fact that, because you get out of the sport as much as you put in, you are ultimately in control of your destiny. Charlotte came fourth at the Beijing 2008 Games, but is proud of the strength of mind required to overcome that enormous disappointment and become a better athlete.

A Golden Dedication

Liz Johnson won her gold medal in the 100m Breaststroke at Beijing 2008 just days after her mother's death, which happened while Liz was on her way to the Games. To Liz, 'The gold medal symbolised everything she'd worked for, as well as me.' The emotional nature of her win means that she would love to defend her title at London 2012. Liz's impressive work ethic has always been one of her strong points. According to her, the pain and effort of training never hurt as much as the pain of losing a race or of some of the other setbacks she has encountered in life, and this keeps her motivated in the run-up to London 2012. As a sign of how much she is respected within British Paralympic sport, Liz was asked to lay the last tile at the London 2012 Aquatics Centre, something of which she is extremely proud.

Legend in his Own Time

David Roberts CBE is an 11-time Paralympic gold medallist and one of Great Britain's most successful Paralympians to date. He was selected to carry the British flag at the Closing Ceremony of the Beijing 2008 Paralympic Games, and this remains one of the highlights of his sporting career – although at the time, the weight of the flag was such that he kept telling himself 'Don't fall.' Despite his extraordinary success, he retains his ambition to keep winning, along with his drive to keep improving. He is much more competitive in the pool than out of it, but, when his training allows it, he also mentors athletes and enjoys motivational speaking. He has also appeared on *A Question of Sport*, pulled a 185-ton aircraft for Comic Relief and addressed the Human Rights Council in Geneva on disabled people's rights.

'I swim like I'm drowning, but
I'm determined never to lose.'

David Roberts

Swimming to Self-belief

David Hill was the the youngest athlete across all
sports at the Beijing 2008 Paralympic Games, at
just 15. Born without his lower arm, he swam and
competed from an early age, and has gained all
his confidence in his life through swimming, so
he says he has a lot to thank the sport for. The
confidence of what he has achieved so far enabled
him, for example, to enrol on a carpentry/joinery
course. It was hardly an obvious thing for him to
do, but he never thought his disability would be an
obstacle. He likes the fact that although swimming
is an individual sport, he trains as part of a squad
at Bath University, and he gets a lot of support and
camaraderie from his fellow swimmers, as well as
a big sense of belonging.

Pushing to the Limit

Nick Beighton is a serving Captain in the British Army with the Royal Engineers. He was injured by a bomb in Afghanistan in October 2009 and lost both legs. In July 2010, as part of his rehabilitation programme at the Ministry of Defence's Headley Court centre, he took up sculling, and his potential was immediately spotted. Nick finds it very empowering to be able to throw himself into a physical activity and push his body to its limits. After the damage done to it, he really appreciates what his body can do – and the harder the challenge the better.

Samantha Scowen had built up a lot of upper-body strength as a result of being in a wheelchair or on crutches since she was a child, and this meant that when she took up rowing, six weeks before the World Cup in 2009, her power and strength were immediately apparent, and she came away from the competition with a gold medal.

Nick Beighton and Samantha Scowen are members of the Great Britain Rowing Team Adaptive Squad, competing together in the mixed Double Sculls. The distance rowed is 1000m, although the Great Britain Paralympic Rowing squad trains over 1500m and even 2000m to give them extra stamina.

Sculling to Success

Tom Aggar is the reigning Paralympic gold medallist
in the Single Sculls, as well as a World Rowing
Championships multiple gold medallist. He used
to swim competitively and played 1st XV rugby for
Warwick University, where he studied Biological
Sciences. In summer 2006, after an accident, he took
up indoor rowing in order to keep fit. At first he had
no coach, but was self-motivated, constantly setting
himself small goals to see if he could improve his
times. Tom soon saw the results of his hard work,
winning his category at the 2006 National Indoor
Rowing Championships. A fiercely competitive rower,
he was selected in 2007 for the Great Britain squad
less than a year after starting the sport, going on to
win a gold medal at the World Championships. His
height and long body give him a long reach and
therefore a useful long stroke.

'It's tough at times, but there's a huge goal at the end of it and hopefully it will all be worth it.'

Tom Aggar

The Fearless Foursome

Members of the Great Britain Rowing squad (from the left), Pamela Relph, Kate Jones, David Smith and Ryan Chamberlain are united in their love of sport. Pamela Relph played basketball and rugby at school, and went on to captain the award-winning cheerleading squad at Birmingham University. 'I was looking for something different to do.' When not rowing, Kate Jones loves other outdoor sports, such as hill walking, kayaking, cycling and skiing. In the past, David Smith has competed for Great Britain in both non-disabled karate and bobsleigh, while Ryan Chamberlain is keen to get back to the mountains he loved to climb before his accident.

Rising to the Challenge

After graduating in Physics from Warwick University, Ryan Chamberlain (seen here carrying his boat in with David Smith) was all set to go to Sandhurst. He took a gap year before starting but was hit by a drunk driver in Bolivia. After numerous operations on his ankle, he eventually had to have his lower leg amputated. He watched the Beijing 2008 Paralympic Games while recovering in hospital from the accident, so is thrilled that he is now himself aiming to take part in London 2012 in the Mixed Coxed Fours. He is now doing a masters at King's College London and trains six days a week, three sessions a day – he particularly enjoys the outdoor sessions on the water. So it's not surprising that, apart from spending time with his girlfriend, he has no time for anything else.

The Art of Rowing

As the son of a rowing coach, James Roe started coxing at the age of 12, and in exchange was offered rowing lessons by some of the oarsmen. Although he is generally easy-going, he admits to being overly competitive when rowing. He finds it an immensely satisfying sport, even the two-hour sessions on the ergo where rowers have to pace themselves to avoid exhaustion. James used to play rugby as a junior but switched fully to rowing at the age of 15 when his eyesight deteriorated. He graduated in Fine Arts from Oxford Brookes University, and continues to enjoy painting and drawing for relaxation because it offers such a contrast to his sport. When he has some spare time, he also coaches at his home boat club in Stratford-upon-Avon.

In Pursuit of Perfection

Kate Jones loves rowing, because it can be so tough. Her motto is, 'If it comes easily, there's no satisfaction.' She first took the sport up as a non-disabled rower at university, where she was studying French and German. Initially, it was just a way of getting fit: it gave her a purpose to go to the gym. Soon, because of Kate's competitive spirit, she discovered that when she was with a group of people who were told to row for a certain length of time, she wanted to be the fastest and the best. She is very strong naturally, is never satisfied with her performance, and always wants to go one better. Since 2009, Kate has competed as a visually-impaired rower, and enjoys the sense of community found at boat clubs so much that she can see herself doing veteran races when she is 60.

The Jeweller who Struck Gold

Naomi Riches' first sport was swimming, and she was a National Disabled Swimming Champion at the age of 12, going on to win gold and silver medals at the London Youth Games at Crystal Palace for four successive years. She did not take up rowing seriously until April 2004, but just four months later Naomi was part of the winning Adaptive Mixed Coxed Four at the World Championships. She raced in the same boat class at the Beijing 2008 Paralympic Games, winning a bronze medal. Since then she has won gold medals at the 2009 World Championships and the first World Cup of 2011. Alongside her sporting success, Naomi has managed to complete a BA in Metalwork and Jewellery Design.

Ruling the Waves

John Robertson, Stephen Thomas and Hannah Stodel love sailing because 'you are not just up against other competitors, you are also fighting against the wind, and having to deal with ever-changing conditions over which you have no control'. John Robertson started sailing at the age of 11 when his father bought a Mirror dinghy. After John's motorcycle accident in 1994 when he was 22, he had to adapt to life in a wheelchair. Sailing, and subsequently representing his country in the sport from 1997 onwards, enabled him to recover his sense of self-worth. He has since won back-to-back Sonar World Championships in the three-person keelboat event, the first crew ever to achieve this, and has now set his sights on a gold medal at London 2012.

Stephen Thomas began sailing in 2002. From being a complete novice, he went on to become Sonar World Champion in 2005 and 2006. This made him realise that nothing was impossible. He especially enjoys sailing in 20+ knots when there are big waves, with the boat planing across the top of them.

Hannah Stodel is highly organised and always thinking ahead. This comes in handy in her role as the crew's tactician, as she has to be able to monitor competitors on the water and anticipate their moves. As the daughter of keen sailors – her mother competed at international level – she has been sailing since she was three years old.

'It's a demanding sport but when you
get it right, it's an amazing feeling.'

Hannah Stodel

Taming the Wind and Water

Megan Pascoe's parents both sailed, so the sport has always been part of her life. In fact, she has been sailing since the age of two. It has enabled her to visit a lot of different places, to make many friends within the huge sailing community, and to challenge her abilities on the water. Megan graduated in 2009 from Bournemouth University with a degree in Sport Psychology and Coaching Sciences, but is driven by the identity she gains from being part of a bigger sailing team. She has a natural talent for learning the kit she is using, and is very consistent in her sailing. Her brother, Sam Pascoe, is a sailing guru – winning the National Championships in the RS600FF, a lightweight skiff with hydrofoils.

Beating the World on Water

Alexandra Rickham hates the cold, and sails in a minimum of three layers. In fact, most people can tell what the weather is like simply by looking at her face. Her ability to stay focused for extended periods is invaluable because, as the helm, she has to concentrate on making the boat go as fast as possible. An environmental scientist by training, Alexandra is currently a full-time athlete: she is making the most of being part of a team, spending her days outside, and trying to achieve something few get the opportunity to do.

Manchester-born Niki Birrell loves the fun, friendship and competition that sailing provides. His father got him into sailing when he was nine years old, his brother also sails internationally, and they are both the biggest influences on his career. Indeed, Niki sometimes takes part in non-disabled regattas with his brother, and one of his proudest achievements was competing with him in the 2005 Team Racing World Championship. The Business and Management graduate is constantly driven to improve, and the focus and determination he displays in his sport, combined with his tactical strengths, have led him and teammate Alexandra to be crowned world champions in the SKUD 18 two-person keelboat event for three consecutive years, from 2009 to 2011.

'Competition has offered me the rush
of adrenaline and the opportunity to
be part of a team again.'

Alexandra Rickham

RACKET SPORTS

Don't Cross the 'Quadfather'

Born in 1960, Peter Norfolk OBE is one of the UK's best-known sportsmen whose outstanding list of titles and achievements includes gold medals at the Athens 2004 and Beijing 2008 Paralympic Games, and 18 majors on the Wheelchair Tennis Tour. Until 2010, he was ranked number one in the world for quad singles for five of the previous seven years. Known for his vicious backhand slice, he only took up wheelchair tennis at the age of 30, and his grit and determination have kept him at the top of the game at an age where many other players would have long retired. Equally, fitness has played an important part in the length of his career, so although he loves good food and wine, he sadly has to forego them in his bid to stay in peak physical condition.

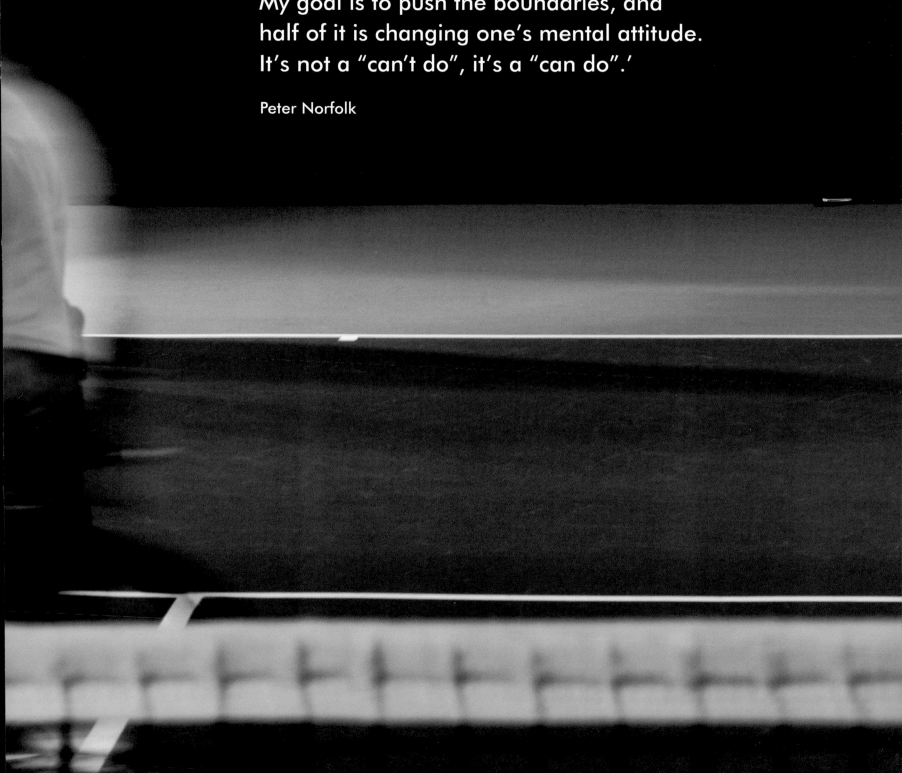

My goal is to push the boundaries, and half of it is changing one's mental attitude. It's not a "can't do", it's a "can do".'

Peter Norfolk

A Radiant 'Royal'

Jordanne Whiley followed the example of her dad, Keith, who won an Athletics bronze in the 100m L3 event at the 1984 Paralympic Games in New York. She took up wheelchair tennis when she was only two years old. In 2007 she became Britain's youngest-ever national women's singles champion aged just 14 and she is now a full-time professional, travelling six months of the year and climbing steadily up the world rankings. She believes the personal thrill and excitement of competing at London 2012 will outstrip her unforgettable experiences at Beijing 2008 and her Grand Slam debut in the Australian Open in 2011. Jordanne is known as 'The Princess' because of her stunning on-court style: she loves big earrings, fantastic coloured nails and brightly-coloured outfits, much like the Williams sisters. She also counts Maria Sharapova and Rafael Nadal amongst her all-time favourite tennis players.

'The motivation of being selected to compete at London 2012 is just so huge. It's my home country and all my friends and family will be watching if I play. Thinking that I could win a medal there is what makes me want to get up and train every day.'

Jordanne Whiley

'Energiser Bunny' Bounds into History

Known for his energy and power game, David Phillipson first took up wheelchair tennis aged six when on holiday in America with his parents, turning professional aged only 15. In 2008 he became the youngest-ever British men's number one, aged just 19. He made his Paralympic Games debut at Beijing 2008, and has won numerous titles in both singles and doubles. Wheelchair tennis allows players two bounces, but otherwise has identical rules to non-disabled tennis. David's strength and his ability never to stop pushing on court come into their own in singles, his preferred event, even though he also enjoys regular doubles success. His motivation comes from the enormous enjoyment he gets from being on court, as well as his love of travelling and of meeting new people – just as well, as he now plays up to 20 tournaments a year.

Garage Gladiator

Will Bayley (seen here playing his fellow Great Britain international Paul Karabardak) was always sports mad, so his grandmother bought him a table tennis table when he was 10 and recovering from cancer. His brother, three years older, used to beat him in most other sports, and this led to lots of arguments! The brothers played for hours after school in the garage and before long Will was beating his brother. Will likens his sport of table tennis to a very fast version of chess, where tactics are as important as speed. Will's drive and determination to succeed mean that he trains for six hours a day, but because he loves the game and competing, he is happy to put in the hours.

Serving up Success

Londoner Aaron McKibbin played table tennis once at school, enjoyed it, and his interest and involvement in the sport carried on from there. He began to play competitively while still at school and, having already become a Great Britain national champion, is proud to be representing his country at table tennis. In July 2011 Aaron won his first international medal, a bronze, in the Team Class 6-8 event. His ambition is now to take part in the London 2012 Paralympic Games and he is devoting all his time and energy to qualifying, including basing himself in Sheffield where the National Training Centre is located. Aaron describes himself as fun, relaxed and committed, and when he is not training or competing, he likes to see friends, listen to music and watch films.

Table Topping Tennis

Paul Karabardak (here playing Will Bayley)
is currently at college studying Welsh. He took up
table tennis at the age of 11 and has been in the
Great Britain squad since 2001, when he was just
15. His strengths include a good backhand block
and drive, great determination, and a love of the
sport that keeps him motivated. He is proud of the
fact that he has maintained a top 15 world ranking
since the age of 19 and hopes that he will be able
to inspire others to achieving their sporting or life
goals. Paul finds time to enjoy other pastimes:
he loves music and films, but his real passion is
following his beloved Swansea City football team:
'We are Premier League.'

Sons and Brothers

David Wetherill's father and older brother both played table tennis, so when he began to play at the age of 10 and beat his dad not long after, he realised he had natural talent. His intense rivalry with his brother also spurred him on, and table tennis has now become his life, although according to David, it is such fun that it makes practice easy. He is doing a Masters in Biological Chemistry at Sheffield University, and enjoys other sports, including swimming and football. David, who plays a fast, attacking game, is hoping to win a medal at the London 2012 Paralympic Games – hopefully gold. He would also love to become number one in the world, having reached number two before a broken arm in 2010 put him out of action for many months. He is seen here playing Aaron McKibbin.

Cool and Committed

Kim Daybell took up table tennis at the age of nine, playing on an old table at home and also at school. He loved the sport from the start, began training more seriously soon after and reached number two in the country by the age of 12. He has always kept himself physically fit and, before committing himself full time to table tennis, he used to play badminton and tennis, and also swam to a high level. Kim is driven by the will to succeed and to perform well under pressure. He began a medical degree at Leeds University in 2011, balancing his demanding studies with high-intensity training in preparation for London 2012.

Fighting for every Point

Liverpudlian table-tennis player Jack Hunter-Spivey will be just 17 during the London 2012 Paralympic Games. Having already obtained eight GCSEs, Jack is taking a year out of full-time college to prepare for the Paralympic Games. One of his strengths is his competitiveness: he will fight for every point, even if he is losing 10-0. He also competes in non-disabled competitions, and enjoys the fact that it makes non-disabled opponents revise their assumptions about playing a very young athlete and also one who is in a wheelchair. He can see their surprise when they realise he can hit the ball back with a vengeance! Jack already does some motivational speaking and coaching of youngsters with disabilities.

Strategies for Success

Ross Wilson took up table tennis on holiday aged seven, and soon afterwards his parents bought him and his sisters a table. He began to practise for hours on end, enjoying the buzz that he received from playing the high-energy sport. Ross also enjoys the tactical element, which is even more important in the wheelchair version of the game than in non-disabled competitions. Ross has been home-schooled since 2010, and soon after he was selected for the ParalympicsGB squad. He is very self-motivated and driven, writing letters to sponsors in order to obtain funding, and spending one week a month at the National Training Centre in Sheffield.

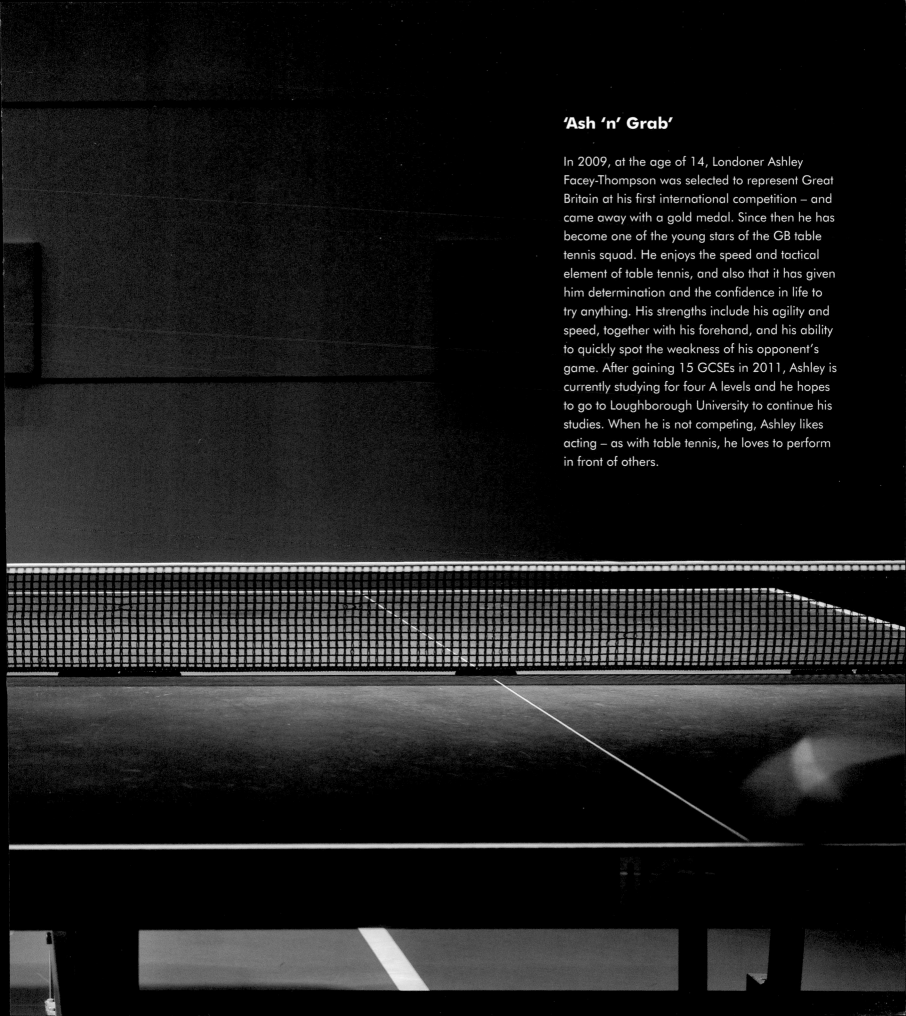

'Ash 'n' Grab'

In 2009, at the age of 14, Londoner Ashley Facey-Thompson was selected to represent Great Britain at his first international competition – and came away with a gold medal. Since then he has become one of the young stars of the GB table tennis squad. He enjoys the speed and tactical element of table tennis, and also that it has given him determination and the confidence in life to try anything. His strengths include his agility and speed, together with his forehand, and his ability to quickly spot the weakness of his opponent's game. After gaining 15 GCSEs in 2011, Ashley is currently studying for four A levels and he hopes to go to Loughborough University to continue his studies. When he is not competing, Ashley likes acting – as with table tennis, he loves to perform in front of others.

A Leading Livewire

Sue Gilroy MBE has won numerous medals playing table tennis at Commonwealth, World and European Championships, and hopes to go on to Paralympic medal success at London 2012. However, she is proudest of being an elite disabled athlete, the number three in the world, British number one, the mother to a daughter and son, and a full time teacher. With a background in science, maths and music, she has taught at all levels, from primary through to degree-level courses. Sue is currently a Year 6 teacher, and also teaches up to 80 children the flute and the recorder. Beyond this, she still finds time to coach table tennis as a volunteer, is patron of a disabled children's charity, Rainbow House, and over the years has helped to raise more than £1 million for it and other charities. Inspired by her parents, she is driven always to be the best she can, and to get the most out of life's opportunities.

Double Ambition

Jane Campbell (left) combines a management-level job in a market research company with full-time training and competing at table tennis, so lie-ins are never an option. She set herself the goal in 2001 to participate in a Paralympic Games, even though at the time she'd never won a single match at international level. But everything she has done in her life since then has brought her slowly closer to her goal. Sometimes she dreams of having a normal life and a day off, but once she starts training, she really enjoys it.

Sara Head (right) originally took up table tennis when she met a boyfriend who played. She took a few sneaky lessons without his knowledge, was instantly hooked, and has kept going ever since. Sara Head's sporting ambition is to compete at London 2012 and she credits her great coach, training partners, family and friends with helping to motivate her to achieve her dreams. She trains full time and most enjoys the multiball drills where lots of balls are hit at her in quick succession, because fast reactions are required and the balls are all different.

COMBAT SPORTS

Getting the Upper Hand

Ben Quilter describes his way of life since taking up judo aged seven as 'strangely addictive'. Judo is a highly technical sport, but Ben, who competes in the -60kg category, thrives on this, and constantly pushes himself to the limit in his thirst for mastering new elements. Although he is right-handed, Ben is left-handed for judo, which is unorthodox and can sometimes give him a competitive edge. A medallist at numerous major tournaments, including gold at the 2010 World Championships, Ben also has a masters degree in Sport and Exercise Physiology. Despite a full-time training schedule, he loves nothing better than relaxing and joking with his fellow athletes, and in particular giving the +100kg judo athletes a bit of grief. 'Everyone likes to get their own back!' he laughs. He is pictured right and overleaf with his throwing partner Lewis Keeble, a member of the Great Britain Judo squad who competes at international level.

'I wouldn't be half the man
I am today if it wasn't for
my sight condition.'

Ben Quilter

Brothers in Arms

Sheer hard work and determination have brought judo athlete Joe Ingram (shown here in white) international success in a very short space of time. Joe, who competes in the −100kg category, only took up the sport in his early twenties, and began full-time training in 2009, aged 26. Judo now gives him everything: his immense fitness, his strength, both mental and physical, his drive and ambition. His younger brother, Sam, is a Judo Paralympian (in the -90kg weight category) and Joe happily admits that, although they remain the best of friends, their rivalry definitely drives him on. Pictured above and overleaf with Joe is Egidijus Zilinskas, a Lithuanian judo international.

'I was not given my ability,
I created it.'

Joe Ingram

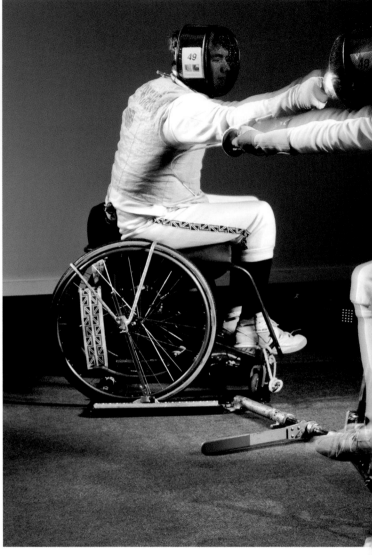

Three Faces of a Fencer

Tom Hall-Butcher (above, centre left and far right), who is studying Ancient History and Archaeology at Birmingham University, has been fencing internationally since he was 16. Tom relishes the thrill and privilege of competing against some of the best in the world, and is proud that he can hold his own against tough competition. He sometimes used to think 'Oh no, what have I let myself in for?' when seeing who his opponent was, but can now tell himself that he is simply facing a big man wielding a pointed stick or sword rather than a multi-medal-winning fencer. It's all part of the growing psychological strength that is underlying his success.

Playing to his Strengths

For many years Simon Wilson (nearest the camera) fenced in non-disabled competitions wearing a prosthetic leg. Then, as Simon recalls, 'a Great Britain coach approached me and said, "Would you be offended if I said you should try the wheelchair version?" He told me my hand-speed was great but I would never be any good because of my lack of mobility.' Fast-forward several years and Simon has set his sights on representing Britain at the London 2012 Paralympic Games.

'I like being part of a squad
and of the fencing family.'

Tom Hall-Butcher

Reflex Action

Justine Moore (left) recently completed her BTEC Sport (Performance and Excellence) qualification, and uses her studies in coaching to help mentor younger competitors. Still only 20, she has won many medals over the years at the National Junior Games at Stoke Mandeville in a range of sports, including table tennis, powerlifting and wheelchair basketball. Wheelchair fencing is her main sport, however, and the one where her fast reactions and strong anticipation skills can be put to best use.

After a career in the police force where she rose to the rank of Superintendent, Vivien Mills (right), who only took up wheelchair fencing after the Beijing 2008 Games, is now a full-time fencer and devotes as much passion and energy to her sport as she used to do to her job. She used to play non-disabled hockey and cricket. The former allowed her to get all her stresses out of her system 'by belting other people's sticks' and she can now do that with wheelchair fencing. In cricket, she used to play wicketkeeper, and this enabled her to develop the hand-eye coordination and fast reflexes that are so vital in wheelchair fencing.

Going Down a Storm

Gabby Down's rise to becoming an international fencer might make even meteors seem slow. Aged 11, she went to a junior games camp at Stoke Mandeville, where she tried out various sports and was immediately talent-spotted by the fencing coach. Within a year she was representing her country at senior international events, and winning gold medals in major competitions. She trains around 10 hours a week after school, and is away most weekends training or competing. Throughout, it is the sheer enjoyment and fun she gets out of the sport that keep her motivated. She never feels stressed and continues to take part in other sports such as athletics and gymnastics. She is shown here facing the camera, in combat with Justine Moore.

'I just have to keep going as hard as I can and see how much better I can be.'

Justine Moore

'What I lack in youth, I make up for in guile!'

Vivien Mills

'I take something away from every competition and then work with my coaches and try and correct it for the next one.'

Tom Hall-Butcher

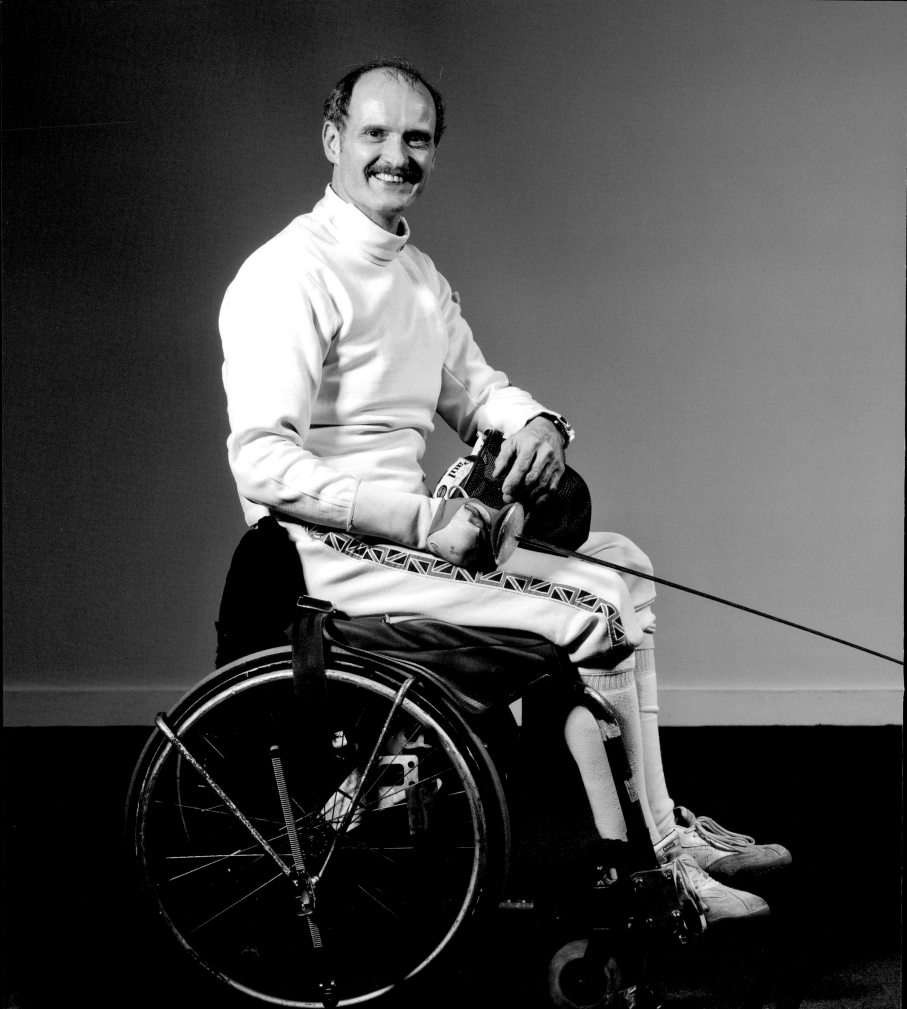

The Perfect Foil

Simon Wilson loves the adrenaline rush from being in a single-man combat situation, which he says can last for days. He describes wheelchair fencing as a 'frantic event', something that he finds immensely enjoyable. Nearly all his fencing is instinctive. It relies on muscle-memory, and on the fact that his body has done each move thousands of times before so that what he produces on the day comes from his unconscious. Born in 1956, Simon is older than most athletes and still works full time, but this motivates him to do everything possible to improve his chances of selection for London 2012. Although he currently has little time for outside interests, he is a massive MotoGP fan, because he rides bikes himself and some years ago raced for one season.

TARGET SPORTS

'Supergran'

Kay Lucas lives and breathes archery. Furthermore, her family does as well: her husband, Kim, is a top-level coach; her daughter, Maia, is also a qualified coach; and her son, Craig, is a keen archer. In 2010, Kay had a fantastic year: she became a grandmother for the first time, she achieved a world ranking of three and she won the European Championships. Her ability to visualise a new shot routine is a great strength of hers, and one of the elements that most appeals to her in archery is the powerful sense of serenity when she completes the perfect shot. Her faith also has a noticeable internal and external effect on her, and is a vital part of her life, both on the field and off it.

Wired to Win

Jemma Morris, who is currently studying for her A levels, loves music and constantly trains with headphones. She has a wide and varied taste in music, but especially likes bands such as Iron Maiden and My Chemical Romance. Jemma took up archery in 2007 and one of the aspects of the sport that appeals to her most is that she can compete and win against non-disabled people. She is proud of being the youngest in the Great Britain Paralympic Archery squad, and is driven by the desire to be the best. Her focus and determination means that her social life and studies have to fit around her training, rather than the other way round.

A Golden Arrow

Law graduate Danielle Brown took up archery in
2003, aged 15. Having done a lot of running and
cycling, illness forced her to give up these sports,
and she became bored being stuck indoors. She
immediately took to the compound bow, and
began to practise every day. She won gold in
the women's Individual Compound competition
at Beijing 2008, and is a World Championships
multi-gold-winning medallist. Yet her biggest
achievement was qualifying for the Commonwealth
Games in Delhi during the same week that
she found out she'd got a first in Law from the
University of Leicester.

'With my disability I had to be mentally strong … I had to develop strategies to cope with the pain.'

Danielle Brown

Bring me Smiles

Pippa Britton (left), who credits her husband with being her biggest support, was born with spina bifida. She has achieved success as a non-disabled and Paralympic competitor. As Pippa says, in non-disabled competitions, 'I sit next to people who stand and hope to beat them. In some cases, I expect to beat them.' It's a very calm sport, not one where adrenaline is of any help. Instead, Pippa has a really strong technical focus, so she knows the fine feel of her equipment, and of what makes a perfect shot. She also spends time during her training doing visualisation work, and stays calm in advance of competitions by reading and doing crafts. She can turn her hand to anything, from knitting and tapestry to making scrapbooks.

Fred Stevens (right) used to be a rifle shooter, but switched to archery after he ended up in a wheelchair as a result of an industrial accident. When he retired aged 65 in 2011, he was the oldest member of the Great Britain Paralympic Archery squad.

In Search of Perfection

John Stubbs has always had good hand-eye coordination. As well as playing snooker recreationally, John played cricket internationally when he was younger before switching full time to archery. Winning a gold medal at Beijing 2008 was, according to him, beyond his wildest dreams. There are very few sports where non-disabled and disabled athletes can compete on an equal level, and this is part of the appeal of archery for John. He shoots six days a week, believing that 'you're never competing against others, you're competing against yourself, striving for perfection.' John is one of the longest-serving members of the squad and is one of the jokers, perhaps because, at the age of 47, he feels he has a bit of perspective on life.

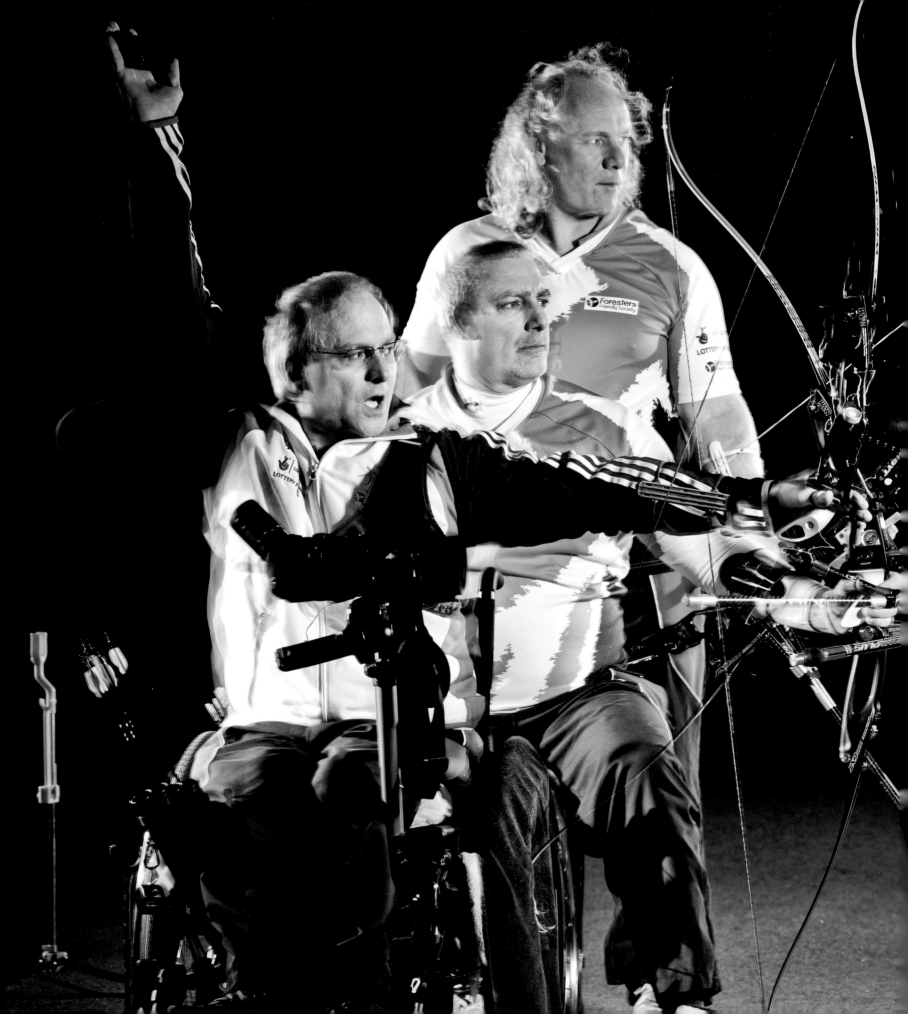

The Three 'Musketeers'

Paul Browne (left) has been practising archery since his school days, but only became competitive years later when he was shown how to string his own bow. This taught him how to take control over his equipment and made him want to learn everything he could about the sport. His dedication paid off and in 2010 he won gold in the 2010 European Championships.

Although Phil Bottomley (centre) comes from Yorkshire, he moved to the Netherlands for work and eventually became a Dutch citizen. When he took up archery, in 2000, he therefore represented Holland, reaching number 4 in the world in his event, the recurve bow. In 2009, he decided to take up British citizenship once more and became part of the GB squad that year. He recently moved back to the UK.

Changing hobby from fishing to archery has given Kenny Allen (right) so much. He has made friends around the world, and has gone on to compete internationally in a mere three years. 'If I can do it at 42, anyone can!' says Kenny. He loves training on a warm, calm, sunny day in the middle of nowhere in peace and quiet. He is less keen when he is shooting on a wet, windy, grey day, also in the middle of nowhere, but with rain dripping off his bow.

Keeping Focused

Pistol-shooter Pam Grainger is very clear that, as well as good hand-eye coordination, the ability to switch off mentally from everything around you is vital in her sport: 'the conscious and the subconscious have to be in sync.' She also keeps fit in order to keep her heart rate down, running and swimming three times a week, and doing strength and conditioning exercises on a regular basis. She only started training properly in March 2010, soon after taking up the sport. Fortunately, Pam, who was a technician in the RAF, says her employers have allowed her to train full time.

A Sport for all Seasons

Adrian 'Bunny' Bunclark likes the fact that shooting can be for anyone: young, old, male, female, disabled or not, all can take part in the same event. Adrian began pistol shooting in 2006 when his wife bought him a shooting lesson as a Christmas present. His talent was immediately spotted and he began competing soon after. He has a lot to thank his wife for, not least her huge ongoing encouragement, and he also feels very fortunate to have found something he has a talent for. He is driven by the fact that he is not as young as other elite shooters, so time is not on his side, but as he is a very competitive person, he performs better when he is chasing a goal.

A Perfect Shot

James Bevis does everything 100 per cent.
Growing up in the country, he has been shooting
guns, especially rifles, since the age of six. He
started taking part in air rifle competitions in 2006,
and he loves the adrenaline of competing and
of winning. He is very driven and perfectionist by
nature, and is constantly making tiny adjustments
to his gun, which is near the 5.5kg weight limit,
because the margins between places can be tiny.
He has even given up full-time work in his quest
for medal success at London 2012, because he
believes that it is only through regular competitions
that he can really know what level he is at.

Nerves of Steel

Nathan Milgate loves taking rifles apart and discussing the minute technical adjustments that could be made to improve their performance. He started pistol shooting aged 16, but switched to rifle shooting because of the gadget element of the equipment. His strength is his consistency, and the fact that he is both quite relaxed and quite analytical. Nathan believes London 2012 will inspire him rather than make him feel excessively nervous or under pressure, and he is looking forward to competing in front of family and friends, and of having the support of the whole nation.

Local Hero

As a child, Matt Skelhon (above and right) enjoyed shooting tin cans and clay pigeons, but he only started competing in 2006. Two years later he left the Beijing 2008 Games with a gold medal, earning him a hero's welcome when he returned to his home village of Stilton in Cambridgeshire; friends and family lined streets decked out with balloons and banners. He has what he calls a 'spontaneous shooting style'. If he thinks about it too much, he doesn't perform as well. Like his teammates, however, his rifle is fine-tuned, down to the contours of his face and cheekbones, in his search for perfection.

'I've got a techie side to me, so I love
the technical aspect of rifle shooting.'

Nathan Milgate

Engineering his Success

David Smith describes himself as 'confident and calm'. Born in 1989, he was just 19 years old when his team won gold in Boccia at the Beijing 2008 Games, a year after Smith became World Champion. His most memorable career moment to date was being on the podium in Beijing, singing the national anthem really badly, with his teammate Nigel Murray in tears beside him! His accuracy and creativity are renowned, as is his all-round technical skill. He trains 16 hours a week and loves every aspect of the training. Furthermore, he is driven by his will to win and the feeling of joy that success brings. Although he is the joker in the squad, David still finds time for the serious business of studying for a degree in Aerospace Engineering at Swansea University and has a particular interest in World War II British military aircraft.

Socks Away!

Born in 1991, Jess Hunter has been playing Boccia for England since the age of 16, and is now part of the Great Britain squad. She loves the competitive element of the sport and the fact that it is within her control. Her strengths are her short game across the court and blasting her opponents' balls out of the way. Jess and her assistant, Lisa, always wear matching socks during competitions, and they have a Hunter team song whenever they go away for training or competitions.

'What do I like about Boccia?
I can do it!'

Jess Hunter

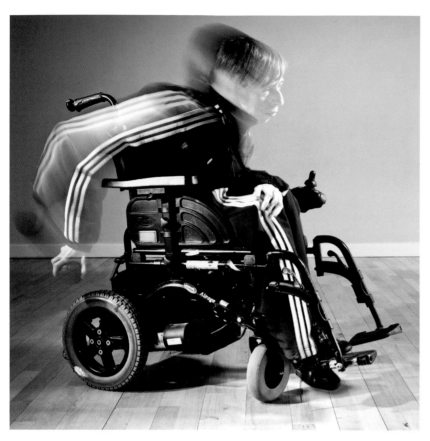 

Boccia Brothers

When Stephen 'Steph' McGuire needed a partner
for the Boccia pairs in 2005 he asked his brother,
Peter (above). Five years later they were winning
silver at the World Championships. Today, both
are dreaming of representing their country at the
London 2012 Games and of winning a medal.
Steph (above right) never tires of his sport, giving
two key reasons: the camaraderie throughout
the Great Britain squad, and the fact that he can
compete on an even level with non-disabled and
disabled people. He understands that tactics,
along with technical skills and a belief in one's
own ability, make the difference between winning
and losing at the highest level.

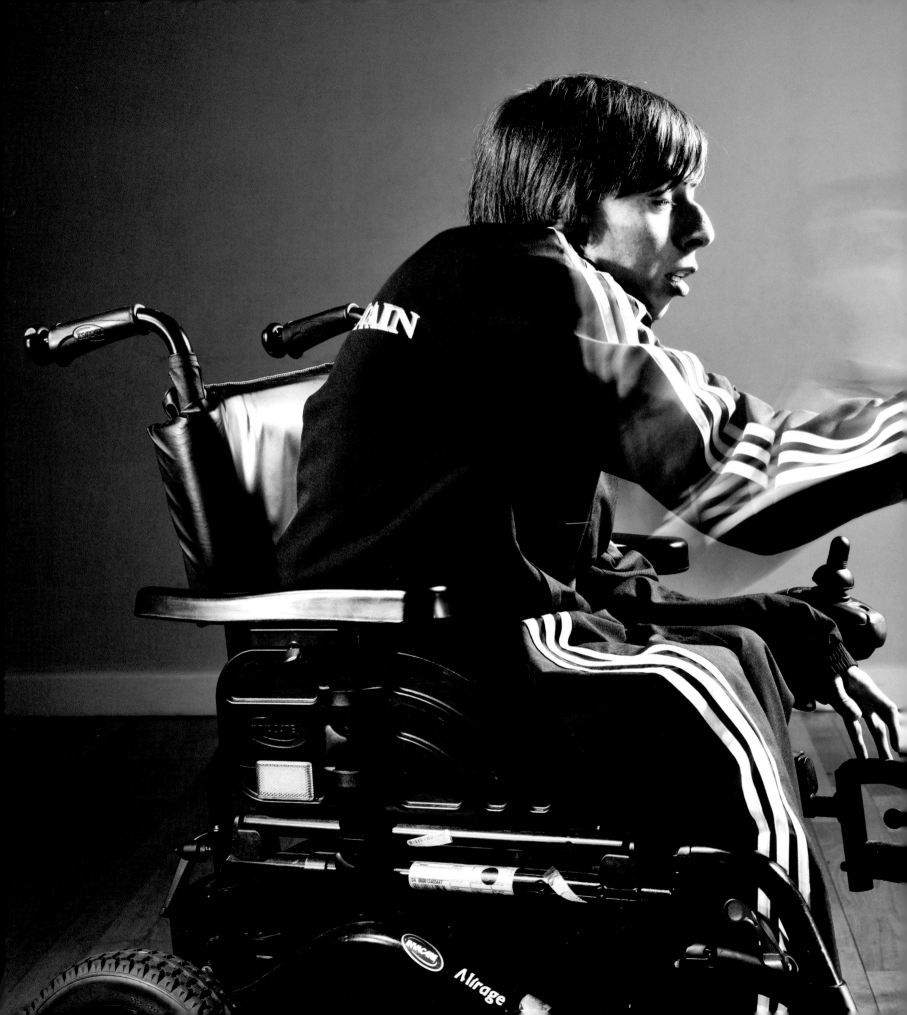

'From the outside Boccia looks simple but it's like a game of chess, every opponent has their Achilles heel.'

Peter McGuire

TEAM SPORTS

The Sky's the Limit

For Mandip Sehmi, to compete at a Paralympic Games is amazing, but to compete in one in his own country, in front of family and friends and everyone who supported him throughout his journey, would be the ultimate sporting experience. Not long after taking up wheelchair rugby, Mandip went on his first international tour, and he was hooked. The tour took him to such far-flung places as San Diego, Singapore, Sydney and Cape Town, and it marked a changing point in his life because it helped him to realise what his limitations were: he had none! After narrowly missing out on a medal place at the Beijing 2008 Games, Mandip is hungry to get on to the podium at London 2012. When he is not training, Mandip tries to find time for his other interests, including football, cooking, music and films.

In the photograph opposite, Mandip can be seen on the right, being chased by his teammate Alan Ash.

A Tidy Mind

Andy Barrow has been in every GB Wheelchair Rugby squad since 1999, winning three European gold medals and taking part in the last two Paralympic Games. 'Few people have the honour of playing for their country, fewer still do so at the Olympic and Paralympic Games, and, as a Londoner, I'm hopefully going to be able to do that in my home town as well in 2012. That means a huge amount to me and would make me feel so proud.' Andy's strengths include his fitness and agility, making him an elusive player when he runs on the ball. As a former hooker in rugby – a sport he remains passionate about – he loves the contact and aggression involved in wheelchair rugby. He admits to being a bit obsessed with tidiness, as anyone who shares his room will attest, thanks to the way he lays out all his kit.

Veterans of the Games

If Alan Ash (left) plays Wheelchair Rugby at London 2012, he will have competed in five Paralympic Games in a row. The icing on the cake would be if he came away from London 2012 with a medal. Alan loves the battle of mind and body during training. He also loves the intense physical competition of wheelchair rugby, which is played between four-a-side teams on a basketball court using a round ball. Although wheelchair rugby is an aggressive sport, Alan's strengths lie in his ability to do just that little bit extra with the ball. He describes himself by using F-words: funny, firm, fair.

An injury while on holiday in Greece meant Steve Palmer (right) was introduced to wheelchair rugby during rehab in Stoke Mandeville, and he left the hospital hooked on the sport. As a result, he now has friends all around the world, and has travelled to places he would never have had the opportunity to visit before, including China during the Beijing 2008 Games. Describing himself as reliable and tough, he is a defensive player and his job is to go round smacking into his opponents' wheelchairs. He creates the gaps for his teammates to go through and score.

'If you smash someone then
it's a great hit. It can get tasty.'
Steve Palmer

'An Awesome Bunch'

So Steve Brown, gold medal winner at the 2007 European Championships, describes his teammates in the tough world of wheelchair rugby. He loves that the squad is focused on being as good as it can, that the players know each others' weaknesses and pull together to make sure that these don't get exploited by opponents. Steve has always been very sporty, doing everything from football and rugby to rock climbing and canoeing, and his accident in 2005 made him determined to become an inspiration to others. Wearing the Great Britain shirt and being captain gives him a double satisfaction: firstly of what he has achieved on a personal level and secondly of being a role model for others in his position, one who can influence their lives for the better. He loves wheelchair rugby and relishes the chance of competing in London before a home crowd: 'Pride. It's all about pride … you want to win.'

The Team to Beat

Winning gold in the 2011 Paralympic World Cup
was the first time Britain's women's wheelchair
basketball team had won any international
competition, and that was a huge confidence
booster for the squad and for Laurie Williams.
Laurie used to do swimming and athletics, but
when she was scouted for basketball she took
to it immediately. She has enjoyed travelling the
world with her sport and meeting new people,
as well as the opportunity to compete at a very
high level. The members of the British squad are
very close, supporting each other and sharing
experiences and emotions. Laurie is one of the
fastest players on the team and is also known for
her defensive play. She manages to combine her
full-time training with a Social Psychology degree
at Loughborough University.

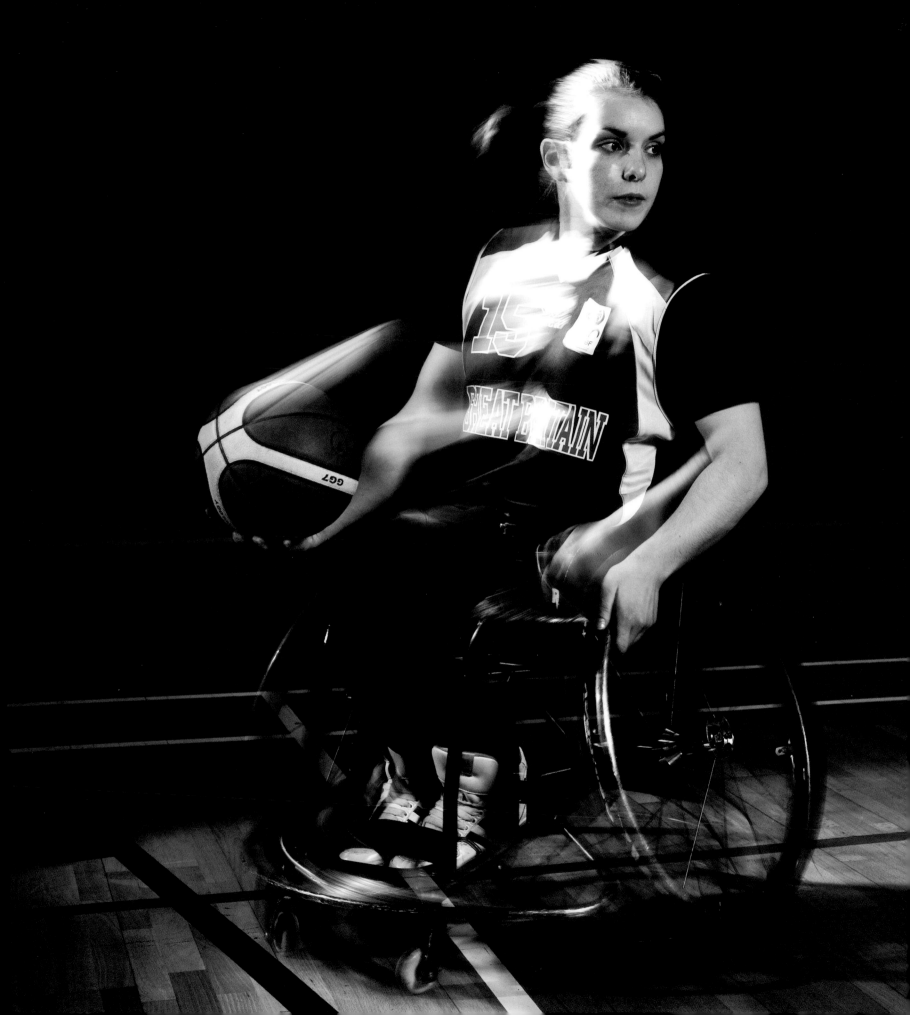

Staying in the Zone

One of Kyle Marsh's strengths in wheelchair
basketball is his shooting. He considers himself to be
very laid back, and his ability to block out negative
thoughts at the critical moment is particularly helpful.
Kyle, pictured above and centre wearing 7 with
teammate Joe Bestwick, took up the sport in 2000,
aged 11; he was playing for the Under-23 team
by the age of 16. In 2010, he captained the Great
Britain squad to their silver medal in the European
Championships, which is his proudest sporting
moment to date.

A Lasting Commitment

Kevin Hayes, a veteran of the previous three Paralympic Games, trains full time, twice a day – as do all members of the Wheelchair Basketball squad. For Kevin – seen here shooting a goal – putting on the Great Britain vest and taking part in the big competitions provide the motivation he needs to keep going. The sport also helps with his everyday life, his mobility, his all-round fitness and health, and he would like to give something back once his playing career is over by becoming a full-time coach.

A Dunkin' Dad

As the father of a little boy, Jonathan Hall is hoping his son will enjoy seeing his dad competing at the next Paralympic Games, saying 'London 2012 will be a massive draw, both for me and for my family and friends.' Wheelchair basketball is the most popular disabled sport in the UK, and is fiercely competitive. Jonathan, who took it up when he was 13, considered it to be more of a hobby until the age of 16. Then, when he got into the full GB squad at the age of 19, he realised that he had to commit to the sport fully. Jonathan is an all-round player, and although he did athletics – and field events in particular – when he was younger, he loves the team element both on and off the court that wheelchair basketball provides.

Seizing the Moment

Lee Manning took up wheelchair basketball in 2005, just before his 16th birthday, when he took part in a taster session at a local club. He loved it straight away, especially the fact that it enabled him to move around fast. Shown here defending the hoop against teammate Joe Bestwick, Lee is 1.98m tall with an arm span well over 2m. He compares himself to Alan Shearer, the former England footballer, saying he has had to work hard to get results rather than rely on sheer talent. He hopes to make an impact in the sport beyond the London 2012 Games, and eventually, after university, would like to be involved in coaching, something he has already begun to do and which he enjoys.

Joe Bestwick believes that sport is an experience to share. He was originally a canoeist, but found he was getting too cold in the boat, so he tried wheelchair basketball. From the age of 16, when he began to really commit to the sport, he has progressed well, pushing himself that bit further and enjoying a real sense of achievement. Although he had begun a Law degree, he now devotes himself full time to wheelchair basketball, on the basis that, although he can always return to education, he can't return to a high-level sporting career.

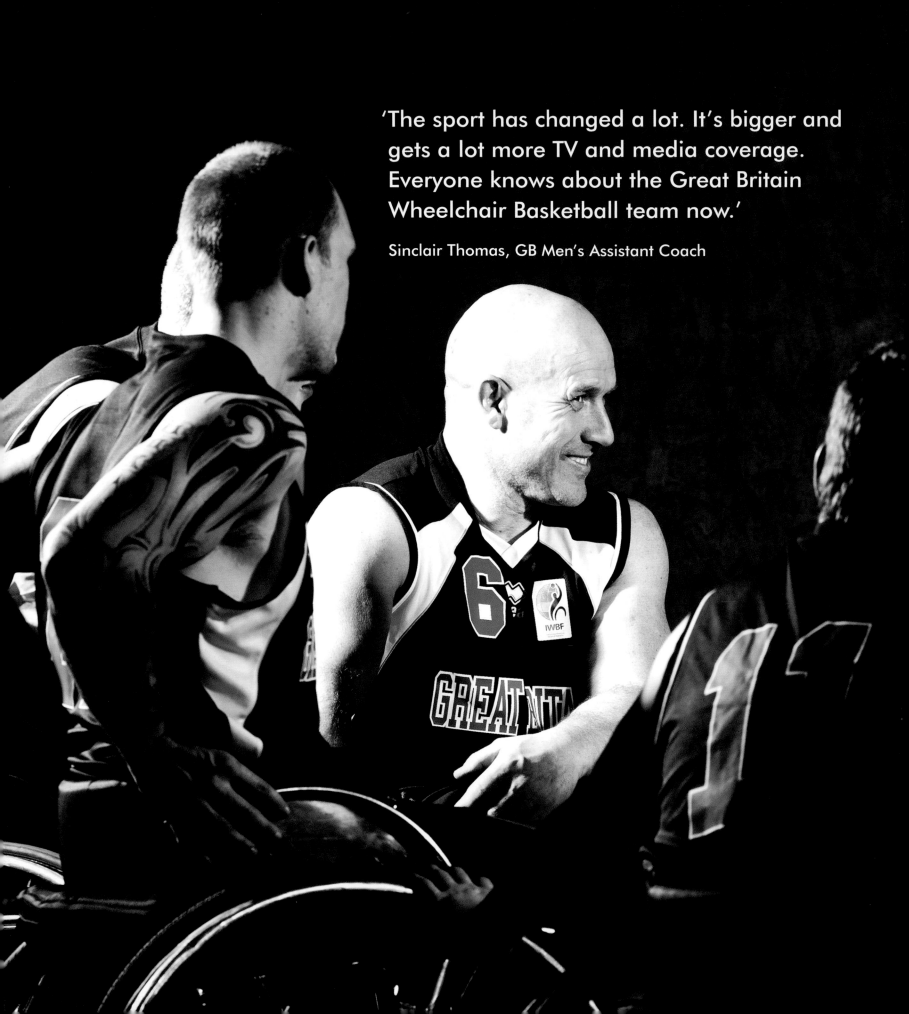

'The sport has changed a lot. It's bigger and gets a lot more TV and media coverage. Everyone knows about the Great Britain Wheelchair Basketball team now.'

Sinclair Thomas, GB Men's Assistant Coach

A Holistic Approach

One of the squad's youngest members, at just
21, Dan English is naturally sporty and used to
swim competitively. He took up 5-a-side football
when at college in Loughborough and the team
manager asked him for a trial. He enjoys the
unique bond that playing a team sport provides,
and the fact that he can share the ups and downs
with his teammates. Dan now trains full time,
but he was part of the way through a degree in
Complementary Therapies, as he is interested in
how they, together with massage, can improve
sporting performance. He hopes to resume his
studies in the future, but in the short term his goal
is to get on the podium at London 2012. Although
he describes himself as laid back, when it comes to
his football, Dan is deadly serious and completely
dedicated. He is seen here passing the ball
towards teammate Jonathan Gribbin.

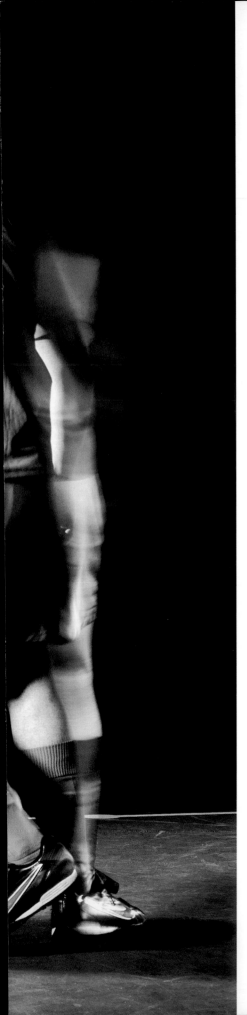

Football 5-a-Side's Gary Lineker

Jonathan Gribbin initially took up tandem cycling when he started to lose his sight in 2005, but when his tandem partner died in a road accident he felt unable to return to the sport and switched to 5-a-side football instead. Having watched football all his life, it was in his subconscious, so he instinctively knew what to do when he got the ball. His quick feet and prolific goal scoring soon led to international success, including selection for the Beijing 2008 Games. When he is not training or competing, Jonathan, seen here with teammate Dan English, works for the FA, visiting schools for the visually impaired in the UK and encouraging the children to take up football.

Just Not Cricket

Keryn Seal played blind cricket internationally for some years before he took up 5-a-side football, and for a while, he managed to juggle commitments to both sports. Eventually he had to give one up, as each one was impacting negatively on the other, and he chose to stick with football because it gave him the opportunity to play at the Paralympic Games and other big events. Keryn, seen here shooting against goalkeeper Lewis Skyers, is a utility player and has played in every position. His strong points are his fitness training and his speed, as well as his commitment and passion. He is a keen Arsenal supporter whose favourite player remains the team's legendary support striker Dennis Bergkamp.

Shoot-out Strongman

For David Clarke, 5-a-side football demands full-time commitment, but he remains a senior partner for Clydesdale Bank, saying 'I'm the last of the amateurs.' David came to 5-a-side football after competing internationally, first in Athletics then in Goalball (he took part in the Atlanta 1996 Paralympic Games). He enjoys football because it is a highly competitive team sport that requires great fitness, skill and a strong mind. David has won five European Championship silver medals and four Golden Boots as the tournament's highest goal scorer, but would dearly love to turn the silver into gold in London.

As the goalkeeper, Lewis Skyers is the one fully-sighted member of the team. He also plays semi-professionally for an 11-a-side non-disabled team and holds down a full-time job. In the past, Lewis has worked as a care worker at a college for the blind, and in the future would like to teach football and other sports to visually-impaired youngsters. Like many fully-sighted people, Lewis was overwhelmed by the quality of 5-a-side football, saying 'I like being with a group of athletes who have that passion to win.'

'The spirit of the Paralympic Games is truly phenomenal. Being in London will be amazing.'

David Clarke

First in Translation

Jessica Luke loves sharing victory as part of a team, and the fact that goalball is a high pace, high intensity and highly tactical sport. The team trained incredibly hard to become the first GB women's squad to win a European gold medal in 2009, which Jessica is incredibly proud of. She recently graduated with a degree in French and Italian from Warwick University, spending a year in Belgium where she trained with the Brussels team. She then obtained a Masters in Translating and Interpreting and is hoping to pursue a career in this field. Jessica loves being able to compete against a wide range of players, be they partially sighted, blind or fully sighted.

Past, Present and Future

Chris Oakley, seen here (nearest to camera) with teammate Joe Dodson, is fascinated by the history of sport. Describing the origins of goalball as a form of rehabilitation for those who had lost their sight during World War II, he says 'something good came out of something terrible, and it shows human endeavour overcoming enormous difficulties'. He believes that part of the responsibility of wearing a GB shirt is to pass on the passion and knowledge to the younger generation. Although always keen on sports as a youngster, especially swimming and athletics, he was never encouraged to compete. Goalball changed all that and gave Chris a lot of confidence; he is now training full time to give himself the best chance of taking part in London 2012.

Joe Dodson, a former manager of a community radio station and freelance radio reporter, loves coffee and poker. He is also a qualified practitioner of neurolinguistic programming, a form of therapy. Joe recently got a new guide dog, Dave, a lovely young retriever, although his previous collie retriever, known as The Bear, still lives with him. He has been playing goalball for over 12 years, since his mid-teens. Joe plays a very fast, attacking game on the wing and can send the ball back extremely quickly; his vicious curling or spinning shots are well known.

'If you want your place you've got to earn it – there are no free tracksuits and no free tickets.'

Chris Oakley (above and right)

Fast, Fit and Flexible

Michael Sharkey (above right wearing 1, with Adam Knott) plays both on the wing and as a centre. Such flexibility is unusual in the sport. As a winger, he has to be very fit and have a lot of explosive power to enable him to shoot the 1.25kg ball very fast from one end of the court to the other. As a centre, he has to have considerable mental concentration and to protect the goal. Michael works as a paediatric physiotherapist in schools for children with learning difficulties. His sister Anna also plays at international level, and trains with him at the gym, which makes things doubly enjoyable.

'It is so exciting to be involved in a world famous competition which everybody … would love themselves to be a part of. I would love to experience the atmosphere at the competition which cannot be paralled with any other experience in life.'

Michael Sharkey

'I get a thrill out of getting hit
by the ball – I don't know why!'

Niall Graham

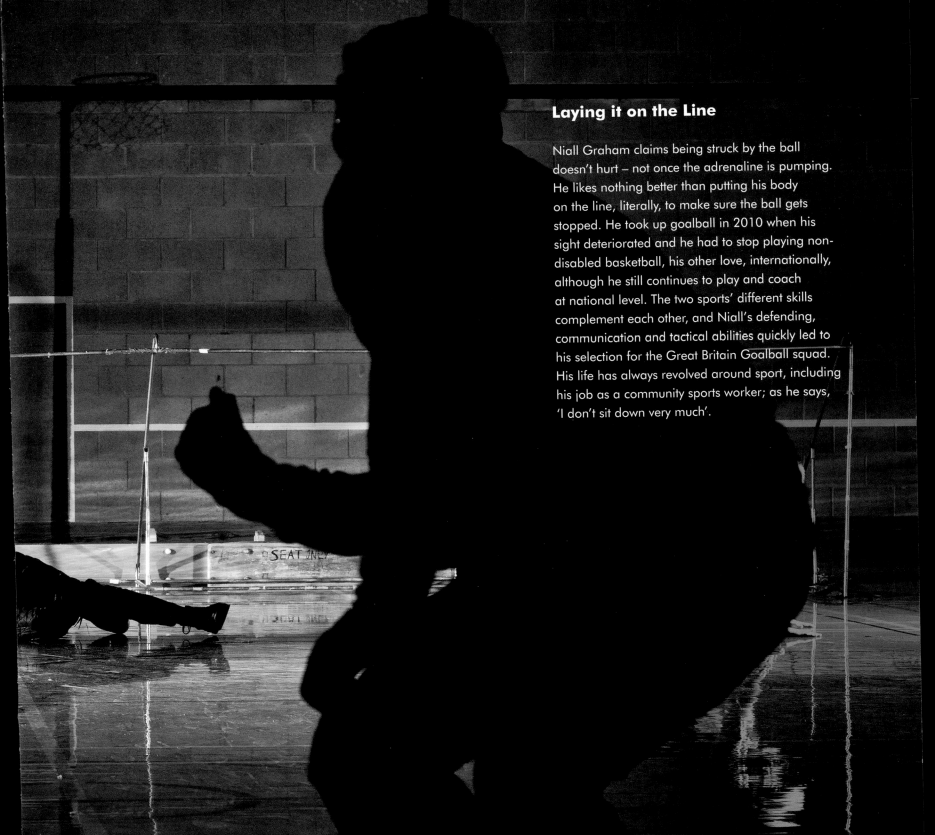

Laying it on the Line

Niall Graham claims being struck by the ball
doesn't hurt – not once the adrenaline is pumping.
He likes nothing better than putting his body
on the line, literally, to make sure the ball gets
stopped. He took up goalball in 2010 when his
sight deteriorated and he had to stop playing non-
disabled basketball, his other love, internationally,
although he still continues to play and coach
at national level. The two sports' different skills
complement each other, and Niall's defending,
communication and tactical abilities quickly led to
his selection for the Great Britain Goalball squad.
His life has always revolved around sport, including
his job as a community sports worker; as he says,
'I don't sit down very much'.

Steering her Team's Success

Louise Simpson, seen here in the centre with her teammates, is proudest of scoring two goals against Finland in 2009 who, at the time, were European champions. Her own strengths are her central defence, and this also requires her to communicate well with her teammates on the wing. Having to be accountable to them is, for her, a positive part of the sport, as is the camaraderie. This is particularly important because goalball is the only Paralympic team sport available to partially-sighted women. When it comes to the long hours of training, which Louise combines with a civil service job, she is driven by the thought of getting stronger personally and as a team. She particularly enjoys the one-on-one training, as it provides quality time to work on improving potential weakness – though she dislikes the stiffness afterwards!

The Beat Goes On

Born in 1995, Adam Knott – seen far right with Michael Sharkey – is the youngest member of the British goalball team. An outstanding musician who has passed Grade 8 in both the piano and the flute, Adam teaches music and is planning to study the subject at university. He sees his future in music and in playing goalball to the highest level possible. He only took up the sport in August 2010, after playing rugby for many years, and also plays visually-impaired cricket for Hampshire, where he is their opening bowler. He took to goalball at once, as it combines the speed and agility of rugby with the technical skills of cricket. On top of all his many commitments, Adam is a season ticket-holder at Southampton FC and tries to attend as many home and away fixtures as he can.

'When I started I didn't have as much padding as I should have. I got a lot of bruises that first weekend, because it's all done on the floor – you have to dive to stop the ball from going in your net.'

Adam Knott

Spike in the Market

Anton Raimondo is a London-based property developer specialising in sourcing unusual or quirky sites that others overlook, and he feels lucky that he can fit in his work around the demands of his sport. His high fitness levels and long arms mean that, although he only took up sitting volleyball in 2009, he is now one of the top all-round players in Britain. He is also calm under pressure and has good analytical skills, which help in such a fast, high-energy sport. Anton enjoys the competitiveness of sitting volleyball, as well as the challenge of pushing back his physical boundaries. He has been a driven person from an early age, largely thanks to his parents' influence, so he is always striving to improve himself not just in sitting volleyball, but in all areas of his life as well.

'I'm motivated by the desire to push my limits, to see how far I can go, to be a part of a team that represents a country and to experience the exhilaration of being in the Paralympic Games.'

Anton Raimondo

A Golden Opportunity

Louise Darby took up sitting volleyball in December 2009, after a severe skiing injury to her knee. She immediately loved the fact that she was able to compete at a high level in a team environment. Core stability and upper body strength are crucial when playing sitting volleyball, though Louise says that the sport takes its toll on players' backsides. She manages to combine training and competitions with her job for Dame Kelly Holmes' company Double Gold Enterprises, where she looks after talented elite athletes for whom mentoring and education days are provided. 'My life is sport,' says Louise joyfully.

'There's a lot of action all the time. You need quick reactions. And then there's an adrenaline kick when you get to hit the ball.'

Anton Raimondo

'I enjoy the speed of the game. It's totally different to all the others I've tried.'

Louise Darby

A Team Built on Talent

Jessica Frezza began serious training for the GB sitting volleyball squad after the European Championships in 2009. This involved three sessions a day, based in Roehampton in London, beginning with the first on-court session at 6 am. Jessica's dedication paid off because she was selected for the World Championships in Oklahoma in July 2010 where the women's team came up against the best in the world, including the reigning Paralympic Games champions, China. Jessica learned a lot from the experience, and the team improved with every game, developing a strong bond and ambition that will stand them in good stead for London 2012.

On Broad Shoulders

Charlie Walker served in the army in the bomb disposal unit until 2008, when he contracted meningitis and lost both his legs. He has always loved taking part in sport, rugby in particular, and his strong build, fast reactions and ball-handling skills made him a natural when he first took up sitting volleyball in 2009. Indeed, the first time he ever played was with the GB squad and they immediately invited him back to train with them the following day. Sitting volleyball is a very active sport requiring high skill and fitness levels. It puts a lot of stress on the shoulders, so Charlie does a lot of gym work to build them up, as well as a lot of core strength work. He's hoping that London 2012 will generate a lot of interest in sitting volleyball. 'It's very fast-paced, there's a good bit of rivalry between the teams and it's a fantastic sport to watch.'

'Oscar Pistorius has a similar disability to me. You see him, see what he's done and you think there are no limits.'

Charlie Walker

FEATURED ATHLETES

Tom Aggar

Kenny Allen

Hollie Arnold

Alan Ash

Andy Barrow

Will Bayley

Nick Beighton

Joe Bestwick

James Bevis

Niki Birrell

Natalie Blake

Phil Bottomley

Pippa Britton

Danielle Brown

Steve Brown

Paul Browne

Adrian Bunclark

Jon-Allan Butterworth

Terry Byrne

Jane Campbell

Ryan Chamberlain

Sophie Christiansen MBE

Josh Clark

David Clarke

Libby Clegg

Felicity Coulthard

Deb Criddle

Jody Cundy MBE

Louise Darby

Kim Daybell

Joe Dodson

Gabby Down

Kyron Duke

Anne Dunham MBE

Nikki Emerson

Dan English

Ashley Facey-Thompson

Jessica Frezza

Sue Gilroy MBE

Niall Graham

Pam Grainger

Dan Greaves

Kate Grey

Jonathan Gribbin

Jonathan Hall

Tom Hall-Butcher

Kevin Hayes

Sara Head

Ashleigh Hellyer

Charlotte Henshaw

David Hill

Jess Hunter

Jack Hunter-Spivey

Bulbul Hussain

Joe Ingram

Ali Jawad

Liz Johnson

Kate Jones

Paul Karabardak

Darren Kenny OBE

Adam Knott

James Ledger

Kay Lucas

Roxan Luckock

Jessica Luke

Lee Manning

Kyle Marsh

Aileen McGlynn OBE

Peter McGuire

Stephen McGuire

Aaron McKibbin

Jenny McLoughlin

Nathan Milgate

Vivien Mills

Justine Moore

Jemma Morris

Rachel Morris

Peter Norfolk OBE

Chris Oakley

Steve Palmer

Megan Pascoe

Josie Pearson

Lee Pearson CBE

David Phillipson

Jo Pitt

Ben Quilter

Anton Raimondo

Pamela Relph

Naomi Riches

Alexandra Rickham

David Roberts

John Robertson

James Roe

Helen Scott

Samantha Scowen

Keryn Seal

Mandip Sehmi

Michael Sharkey

Emma Sheardown

Vicky Silk

Louise Simpson

Matt Skelhon

Lewis Skyers

David Smith (Boccia)

David Smith (Rowing)

Nathan Stephens

Fred Stevens

Hannah Stodel

Sarah Storey OBE

John Stubbs

Owain Taylor

Stephen Thomas

Sinclair Thomas

Charlie Walker

David Weir MBE

Sophie Wells

Dan West

David Wetherill

Jordanne Whiley

Laurie Williams

Ross Wilson

Simon Wilson

Bethany Woodward

Author's Acknowledgements

I would like to thank the following for all their help on this book:

Ann Cutcliffe OBE, Vice-Chair of the British Paralympic Association, for all her support and help to complete this wonderful book; Sally Smith – for her vision; the British Paralympic Association; London Organising Committee for the Olympic and Paralympic Games (LOCOG); UK Athletics; Disability Sport Wales (FDSW); Archery GB; GB Boccia; British Cycling; British Dressage; Royal National College for the Blind (RNCB); British Judo; British Weightlifting; Disability Target Shooting GB; Volleyball England; British Wheelchair Basketball; British Disabled Fencing Association; Disability Tennis Federation (Disability TF); British Table Tennis Association for Disabled People (BTTAD); Royal Yachting Association (RYA); British Swimming; and Hannah Hore, Definitive Sports.

Plus the team to get this all together: Sarah Williams; Brendan Mcilhargey; James Osborne; Shaun Smith; Debbie Beckerman; Briony Hartley; Sarah Blankfield; and last but not least Catherine Bradley – my inspired editor at John Wiley & Sons.